On Your Bike
in
Norfolk and Suffolk

Tessa West

GW00514880

COUNTRYSIDE BOOKS
NEWBURY, BERKSHIRE

First published 1998
© Tessa West 1998

COUNTRYSIDE BOOKS
3 Catherine Road
Newbury, Berkshire

ISBN 1 85306 517 X

Designed by Graham Whiteman

Photographs by the author
Maps by Roland West
Front cover picture supplied by
Cyclographic Publications

Produced through MRM Associates Ltd., Reading
Printed in Singapore

CONTENTS

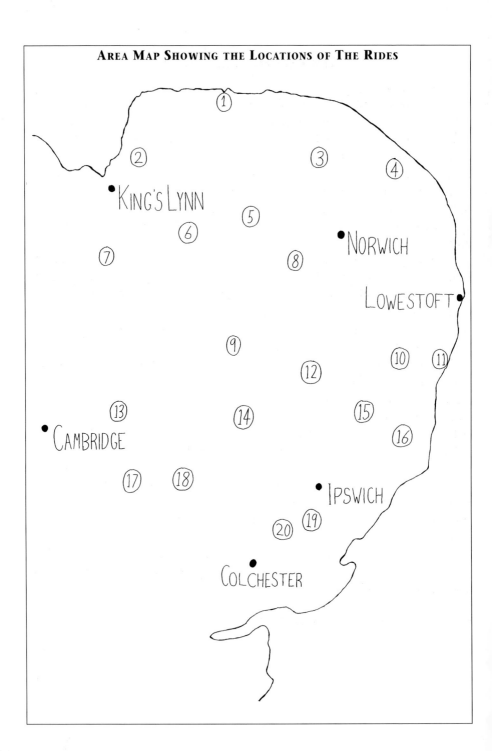

AREA MAP SHOWING THE LOCATIONS OF THE RIDES

INTRODUCTION

This book is intended to make you eager to get a bike – new or old, it doesn't matter – and jump into the saddle. You are invited to explore new places, breathe fresh East Anglian air and take enough exercise to make you work up a thirst which you can slake at one of the many pubs or tea rooms that you'll pass on the routes described here. Compared with many other hobbies cycling is inexpensive, suitable for all ages and something for which you need no expertise. Although many people like to cycle with a companion, plenty of others enjoy setting out on individual adventures.

East Anglia is ideal cycling territory. All of the twenty routes detailed here take you through delightful – and predominantly flat – countryside in Suffolk and Norfolk. A few venture into Cambridgeshire and Essex. All of them take you to interesting villages or small towns. Each route has been worked out so that it starts and ends in the same place, includes several interesting features and, except on infrequent occasions, uses minor roads.

Not only is this region easily accessible, but it has beautiful countryside and fascinating old buildings. It's impossible to ignore the churches, guildhalls and manor houses that were built by wealthy and influential individuals and groups who lived here hundreds of years ago. Seen from behind a steering wheel these pass in a flash, but if you are on a bike you get a far better sense of their construction and place within the community.

The routes vary in length from 13 to over 25 miles. Almost everyone, even without trying, cycles at about ten miles an hour. Believe me, it's really easy to cover the miles, and even if you want to stop every hour for ten minutes and then take a couple of longer breaks to watch boats, snooze or have lunch, a route of 25 miles will only take you around three and a half hours. That means that if you set off at, say, 10.30, you'll be in the saddle for about two and a half hours, out of it for an hour or two, and back where you started by three o'clock.

So, which ride will you do first?

Tessa West

GUIDE TO USING THIS BOOK

Each route is preceded by information to help you:

The **route title** tells you the main places that you will start from or pass through. Because some cyclists will arrive at the starting point by car each route ends where it begins. However, of course it's possible to start and finish the route wherever you want.

The **number of miles** is the total for the ride. All the rides are along roads which, unlike some tracks, can be ridden at any time of year.

The brief **introduction** to the ride gives a broad picture of where the route goes and also mentions particular features that you will see. The introduction is where you will find out whether the route takes you across or along any main roads. It will also indicate if heavier traffic is likely in summer.

The **maps** listed at the beginning of each ride are all Ordnance Survey maps and it is advisable to take them with you as the route maps give limited information.

The **starting point** names a village or town and gives its location in East Anglia in relation to other towns and to main roads. Many routes give a specific starting point within the town or village, This is usually, but not always, a car park.

Places for refreshment, sometimes particular pubs or tea rooms, are mentioned in the pre-ride information, but you will find more places listed in the text about the ride. And others are just waiting for you to discover them. Don't forget Paragraph 211 of the Highway Code: You MUST NOT ride under the influence of drink or drugs.

Very few rides in this area are really hilly, but some indication is given **about ups and downs**.

THE ROUTES

It is a good idea to read right through a route before setting out so that you note any places where you want to spend more time. The routes have been arranged according to their position in East Anglia rather than to their length or difficulty, so just choose ones you like the look of.

Each route itself is set out in blocks of only a few lines. This is so you can find your way around the page easily. The directions have been written as clearly as possible. Instructions to turn left or right are printed in bold, like this: **Turn L** at the T-junction, or **bear R** when the road forks by the church. Instructions to continue straight over a crossroads or carry straight on are not in bold.

The directions include some description about the route, but at the end of each route there is more information about **places of interest**. These include notes about architecture, history, legends and people connected with each entry.

The map of East Anglia on page 4 shows where the twenty routes are situated. Each route is accompanied by a simple **sketch map**. These maps are intended to give you a general idea of where the routes go but are not detailed enough to be route guides. The relevant OS Landranger Series map is always recommended.

SAFETY
Make sure that your bike and those of any companions – especially children – are roadworthy. This book is about routes not repairs, so seek elsewhere for do-it-yourself information or a good bike mechanic. It is unwise to set off knowing that, say, your gears are not working properly or your saddle is too low. Get things checked before you go, especially if you are riding an unfamiliar bike.

Decide in advance what you are going to do if your bike gets a puncture, and be prepared. There is no point in equipping yourself with a puncture outfit if you don't know how to use it. It might be better to take a spare inner tube – plus the tools you'll need – but of course you'll need to know how to deal with this, too. A mobile phone might be the best insurance policy, assuming that there is someone to phone who is

prepared to come and rescue you.

Make sure you don't have things dangling off handlebars or panniers.

Locking your bike will be completely unnecessary in most of the places these routes take you but use your common sense and lock if in doubt.

Safe cycling
Wear comfortable clothes and shoes. Wear a helmet.

Stop if you want to consult a map or this book, otherwise you may ride into a car or a ditch.

If you are with someone else or a group make sure that the pace suits everyone, and arrange that those who are ahead will stop at intervals to give the others time to catch up and get their breath before setting off again. If you are one of the fastest don't forget that the people behind you may not be so fit, so practised or so fond of cycling as you are. Look after them.

If you find yourself cycling in traffic you may feel safer to walk and push your bike, even if you extend your journey by half an hour.

Riding after dark is dangerous even with lights. Be very careful if you do so.

1

Wells, Walsingham and the Burnhams

22 miles

This route is in the most northerly part of Norfolk, right on the edge of East Anglia. The ride takes you along a coastline that keeps its distance from the sea. Wells-next-the-Sea is no longer quite as close to the sea as its name suggests, but nevertheless the nautical theme is constantly reinforced by the frequent reminders of Lord Nelson, whose birthplace you'll pass in Burnham Thorpe.

Little Walsingham introduces a completely different culture, for its shrine is famous amongst pilgrims, and tired pilgrims have much in common with tired cyclists, so you should find food, drink, peace and solace there. Be sure to enjoy Wells before you go home.

Map: OS Landranger 132 North West Norfolk (GR 916438).

Starting point: Wells-next-the-Sea, which is on the A149 just at the top of East Anglia's northern bulge, about 10 miles north of Fakenham. Wells is very busy in the summer and though there are plenty of car parks, they soon fill up.

There are various pubs in the Burnhams but a good place to have lunch and renew your energy might be the tea rooms in North Creake. The second part of this ride can seem a longish haul if you are hungry.

Be prepared for a few hills once you are away from the coast.

The B1105 towards Burnham Market runs right next to the harbour and, from a position facing the sea, you need to **turn L** onto it.

After a mile you will join the A149 at a sharp bend. **Turn R** onto it and ride for 1½ miles until you reach the Victoria pub by the entrance to Holkham Hall. **Turn L** into the roadway that leads to the Hall.

The road leads you under an arch and into Holkham Park. Follow the road round so that you pass in front of the house and along one end of the lake. Keep going and **take the right hand fork** when the roadway divides. Ignore the next turning to the left but keep going to the back exit from the Hall grounds which you will reach after 1½ miles.

Cross the lane to join the B1155 again, and **turn L** onto it.

Follow this road for about 2 miles to Burnham Overy Town. You will see the church on your right, and soon after that **turn R** at the T-junction, onto a minor road which takes you to Burnham Overy Staithe. Here beside the harbour there's a pub called the Hero – one of the many in this part of Norfolk that are named after Lord Nelson.

Then return along the same road to

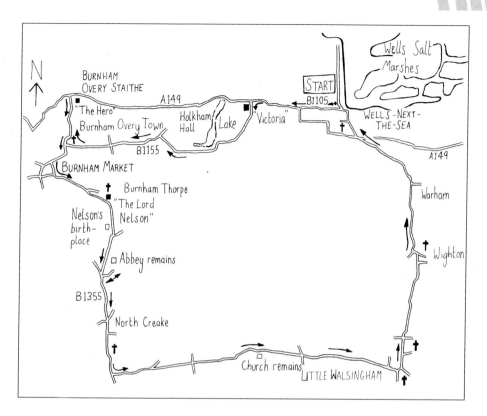

Burnham Overy Town, past the Lord Nelson, and join the B1155 towards Burnham Market.

Go through Burnham Market and then **turn L** onto a road signposted to Burnham Thorpe. Ride for 2 miles and you'll come into the village where Nelson was born. **Turn L** down a lane towards the church and you'll see Nelson's special White Ensign flying. See the note on the door. Return to where you turned down to the church and **turn L**. Go past the Lord Nelson pub and find Blacksmith's Lane on your right. It's nearly opposite the road to Burnham Overy. **Turn R** here.

In less than a mile pass the site of the parsonage where Nelson was born, marked by a plaque in the wall on your right.

Then ride on, **bearing R** at the fork, until you meet the B1355. If you want to see the remains of Creake Abbey turn left here, down a track.

Then rejoin (if you left it) the B1355 and ride into North Creake. Look out for the post office and tea rooms on your right – this could be a good place to stop if you've had enough of Nelson.

Pass the church on your left, and carry on until the crossroads where you **turn L** towards Little Walsingham.

Go up the first hill and keep going steadily. You have several miles ahead of you of straight roads which have a few more hills. Cross over the crossroads and pass the ruined church on your right. Cross over

Holkham Hall.

another crossroads and then ride the final couple of miles into Little Walsingham.

Because Little Walsingham is the destination of pilgrims you will find plenty of places of refreshment. Leave your bike somewhere · and enjoy wandering around the churches – there's even a Russian Orthodox church – and little back roads. As well as tea shops you'll find the Bull Inn and the Black Lion.

Later, set off again from the little green with the memorial cross along the road signposted to Wighton and Wells. Do not take the road back towards Egmere and South Creake.

This road runs parallel to the railway line and you will be in Wighton after 2 miles. As you come into the village, **turn R** down a lane if you want to visit the Sandpiper pub and the art gallery. Otherwise follow the road round to the left towards Wells.

You will reach Wells after 3 more miles. when you meet the A149 **turn L** onto it and then **turn R** into the town centre.

NELSON AND THE BURNHAMS

Horatio Nelson was born in a parsonage at Burnham Thorpe in 1758. He went to sea when he was 12 years old and grew up to fight great naval battles, the most famous of which was at Trafalgar. In London, Nelson's statue stands on the column in Trafalgar Square, and his coffin is in St Paul's, but here in Norfolk he is remembered in the names of pubs and by the White Ensign that flies above this village church and is not allowed to be flown anywhere else. Burnham Overy Staithe was once a busy port with barges and schooners, but now it's a place for weekend boat lovers. Burnham Market, which comprises several mini-Burnhams – Burnham Westgate, Burnham Sutton and Burnham Ulpf – is the biggest of the seven Burnhams united by their proximity to the River Burn, although Burnham Deepdale is now separated from the others because the course of the river has altered over the years.

LITTLE WALSINGHAM

This beautiful little town has become a place of pilgrimage because in 1061 a noblewoman, Lady Richeldis, had a vision of the Virgin Mary here. She decided to have built a replica of the house in Nazareth at a place where a spring appeared as predicted in her vision. The shrine became a popular place and, as time passed, was visited by more and more people – including every monarch from Richard I to Henry VIII. It even became known as 'England's Nazareth' and it currently attracts about 100,000 pilgrims each year, some of whom make the final part of their journey in bare feet.

2

Sandringham

20 miles

This is a royal ride through the Queen's Norfolk country estate. It takes you through beautiful woodland and parkland and to Wolferton railway station which was used by the royal family before the railway was closed. If you do not have time to visit Sandringham House and gardens, make sure you call in at the little church with its special atmosphere and exquisite silver work on the altar and pulpit.

The route also takes you out to the east of the estate into rolling, wide country that epitomises Norfolk, and at one point you will be rewarded with a panorama of the fertile land crossed by Celts and Romans.

Map: OS Landranger 132 North West Norfolk (GR 690288).

Starting point: The Visitor Centre at Sandringham Country Park. Sandringham is about 8 miles north of King's Lynn just off the B1440 to the east of the A149 which runs between King's Lynn and Hunstanton.

The Visitor Centre has attractive shops and tea rooms and is a good place to have a pre- or post-ride drink but it's very crowded in summer. This is the only ride that passes no pubs at all, so your best plan for lunch is probably a picnic.

There are some hills on this ride. None of them is steep, but some are longish.

A path from the Visitor Centre leads across a road to Sandringham House itself. **Turn R** onto this road by the memorial cross on a green, past wide verges usually occupied by parked cars. **Bear R** at the fork, keeping on your road. You will pass a noticeable house called The Folly on your right and then meet the A149. Cross straight over this, carefully.

Ride on through lovely woodland and stay on your road when you reach a diagonal crossing, by continuing straight over. The road leads you into Wolferton, past the church on your left. Keep your eyes open for the disused railway station and its museum on your left. Note the village sign, a reminder that the sea is very close and was

once even closer.

Follow the road round and up a hill and back into the woods.

Cross straight over the same diagonal crossroads and carry on to the A149. Cross over here and continue through the woods, straight over another crossroads and on for a mile until you meet the B1439.

Turn L here and ride into West Newton, a pretty village with its church up on your left. **Turn R** at the crossroads, onto the B1440. Ride along here, noting the tall water tower across the fields to your left, and the ruins of a church. Just over 1½ miles (from West

The gates at Sandringham House.

Newton), **turn L** along a lane. At the T-junction **turn R** into Flitcham.

The church is down a little roadway to your right. In the centre of the village **turn L** onto Anmer Road, the B1153. This takes you uphill for well over a mile. At the top of the hill take the **L turn** down a minor road towards Anmer, but before you do so stop and take a look at the splendid view behind you.

After a mile or so you will come to a T-junction. **Turn R** here, and then immediately **L** towards Shernborne (unless you want to see Anmer church which is up a lane opposite the road to Shernborne).

The road to Shernborne is long and straight. Just keep going for over 2 miles until you reach the little low church that tells you you've arrived in the village. **Turn L** here on the road signposted to Dersingham.

After 2 miles **turn L** at the crossroads and, half a mile further on, cross over the small crossroads and ride through the woods back into the Sandringham Estate. **Turn R** when you meet the B1440 and you will come back, past the elegant, stately wrought iron gates of Sandringham House, to the Visitor Centre which will be on your right.

SANDRINGHAM

This country house was bought in 1862 by the future King Edward VII. Although he had many structural changes made it remains a house rather than a palace. It has 85 acres of gardens which you probably won't have time to see if you are going for a bike ride, but you should make time to look at the little church attended by the royal family when they are in residence. The church is quite different from any other village church or, at least, different from any other in this book. You cannot fail to be impressed by the ornate gilded roof and by the stunning silver altar and pulpit front.

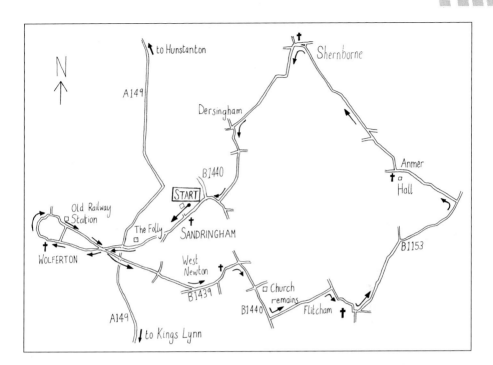

WOLFERTON

Wolferton became well known after Prince Edward bought Sandringham, because all royal visitors to the estate arrived here by train at the small railway station. But the last royal train ran in 1966, and three years later the branch line was closed. Now the former station houses a particularly interesting museum containing many of the original furnishings used by the royal visitors who had refreshments there while their luggage was conveyed to Sandringham House. This museum is worth stopping for, but be prepared to spend longer there than you intended. However, even if you do not go in, you can see from the road the station platforms and the grassy railway track between them.

(3)

Blickling and Reepham

24 miles

This route takes in Norfolk's most renowned stately home, Blickling Hall. It looks as good as new – perhaps better – and it's easy to imagine horse drawn carriages driving up the wide drive. A few miles further on you can see the exquisite church at Salle, and then call in at Reepham where you are likely to want to stop, explore and seek some early refreshment. Don't miss Reepham's former railway station where there are shops, a café built on the platform and a small museum of toys and household items from the last 50 years. If you have not got a bike you could hire one here and adjust the route accordingly. You'll pass Mannington Hall with its moat and drawbridge before continuing along minor roads that lead through Norfolk's heartlands and back to Blickling.

Map: OS Landranger 133 North East Norfolk (GR 156353).

Starting point: Blickling Hall. This is about 1½ miles north-west of Aylsham on the B1354. There is a big car park here that gets full in summer, and there's a pub, the Buckinghamshire Arms.

There are plenty of eating places in Reepham, both pubs and tea rooms, but keep a space for when you are in Heydon when you'll be just about halfway.

It's a ride in and out of little villages and towns, and has a few ups and downs even though you follow the course of the River Bure which is making its way to the Norfolk Broads.

As you come out of the car park onto the B1354 **turn L** and then, opposite the church, **R** to Silvergate. Keep straight on, leaving the triangle of grass on your right and then **bear R** just past Abel Heath Farm and then **R** again.

After about 2 miles you will reach a crossroads. **Turn L** here towards Cawston and ride through Oulton Street. Ride on until you reach the B1149. Cross straight over and ride into Cawston, **turning R** and then **L** down Booton Lane to see the church with its famous tower, Plough gallery, hammerbeam roof and its wodewose or wild man carved above the door.

Go back up Booton Lane and **turn L** onto the B1145 and continue for another 3 miles into Reepham, noting but not taking the turn to Salle on your right. **Turn L** just past this, on the road signposted to Alderford and then immediately **R** at the Crown. **Turn R** by the Spar shop and enjoy wandering around Reepham.

When you are ready go back up to the B1145 and cross over to the railway station. When you come out **turn L** out of the station and then **L** again, along the road to Salle.

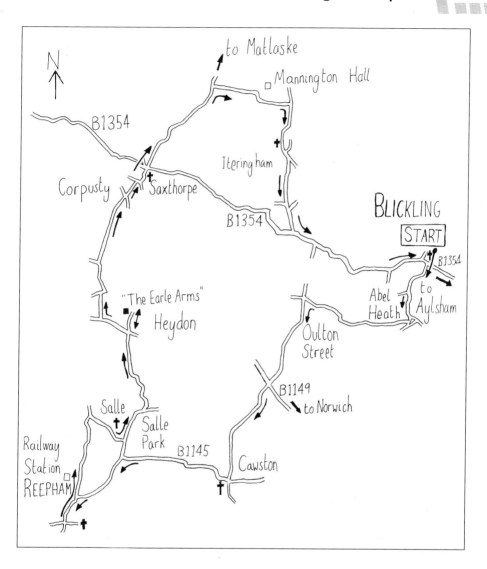

Ride for almost 2 miles and **turn R** when you see the sign to the church. Salle church, built from the profits generated by the wool trade, is exquisite. It's more like a small cathedral standing in a field beside a tiny village.

Ride on past the church and then **turn L**. Ride along the side of Salle Park and take the **L turn** towards Heydon. Cross over the diagonal crossroads and straight into Heydon, a delicious traditional village where you can relax on the green, and eat and drink in the Earle Arms or in the Heydon Stores. This shop not only has its original counter and wooden drawers but also a pleasant tea room and garden.

This is a no through road so you'll have to turn round and go back to the road you were on and then **turn R** and next **R** towards Corpusty.

Keep going for another 2 miles and cross over a small diagonal crossroads, making for Edgefield and Holt, just before you reach Corpusty. Ride across the former railway track and into the centre. Once across the River Bure by the watermill, you'll be in Saxthorpe.

At the road junction by Saxthorpe church and the Dukes Head cross straight over, carefully, onto a minor road towards Matlaske. After a couple of miles **turn R** to Mannington Hall. You can see the gardens and the moated manor house on your left.

Turn R at the next T-junction, signposted to Iteringham. Go straight through the village and cross the bridge over the River Bure by Iteringham Mill – a pub. **Bear R** when the road forks and **turn L** onto the B1354.

Blickling Hall is just over 2 miles further on, on the left-hand side.

BLICKLING HALL

This exceptionally beautiful stately home was built between 1619 and 1628 on the site of a medieval manor house. The National Trust now owns the house and its gardens. As you may not have the time or energy to do them justice before or after a bike ride you should resolve to return to them and also to Mannington Hall on another day. But at least take time to admire the red brick façade of the Hall which faces the road. It looks almost exactly as it would have done 350 years ago but try to imagine it without the wooden clock tower – this was not added until 1830.

REEPHAM

If you are asking directions, you need to know that this place is pronounced *Reefham*. But however you say it, Reepham is worth pausing in. There are little streets running around the two and a half churches that are hardly separated. Other buildings to notice are the Kings Arms, the Old Brewery House with its sundial and the Bircham Institute. Keep your eyes open for the old cycle advertisement on the wall near the Spar shop. You should take a stroll in the Market Square, especially on Wednesday when it's market day. The former station now houses a shop, café and museum. It also hires out bikes.

(**4**)

The Broads

22 miles

This ride could almost tempt you to sell your bike and buy a boat. Because the Broads are so special and therefore attract masses of visitors, this route tries to send you along minor roads but it will also introduce you to some of the most famous places like Potter Heigham and Horning. Most of the Broads are surrounded by marshes and reeds so although you cannot ride along the water's edge you'll see fields with more swans and sails than cows. Why not spend at least an hour of your day having a boat ride as well as a bike ride?

You may just find that you want to drink outside little pubs and watch what happens on the water. But riding between these liquid attractions is good too.

Map: OS Landranger 134 Norwich and The Broads (GR 370252).

Starting point: Stalham, which is on the A149 about 6 miles south-east of North Walsham. The car park is just off the main road on the North Walsham side of the village. Stalham is situated to the north and less popular part of the Broads and has been chosen because parking elsewhere can be very difficult in the summer.

The Broads are peppered with pubs – you'll be spoiled for choice. But they are all there because of the many visitors, so try not to do this ride on a weekend in the middle of summer. Beware too of the roads, for at times the traffic on them can be as busy as traffic on the water. This ride avoids main roads wherever possible, but you will have to go on them for a mile or two on several occasions, notably at the start.

Some of the route is only just above sea level, but it's not as flat as a pancake.

Turn R onto the A149 out of Stalham, towards North Walsham. After 2 miles you'll cross Wayford Bridge. Just under a mile further on **bear L** onto the A1151 towards Wroxham.

Turn L off this road at the first crossroads and continue into Neatishead. **Turn L** opposite the White Horse, towards Irstead. **Turn R** just before the Barton Angler and then **R** at the T-junction.

Turn R at the next turning and follow the winding road through the village. Then cross over the crossroads, signposted towards Hoveton church.

Take the next **R turn** towards Horning. Then **turn L**, still going towards Horning. In a little while you will see RAF Neatishead on your left. Cross over the crossroads and you will come to the A1062.

Cross straight over Lower Street which takes

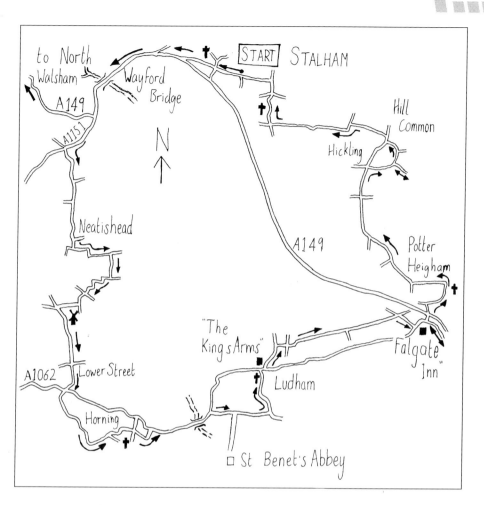

you into Horning and its staithes and several pubs by the water. Enjoy looking around here before continuing along Lower Street.

Turn R if you would like to visit the Ferry Inn and boatyards. Otherwise continue straight along the road you are on past Horning First School and then over a small crossroads, and then follow the road sharply to the left to arrive back at the A1062.

Turn R onto the A1062 and continue. You will cross Ludham Bridge and see a windpump on your left. **Turn R** down a

lane by the pub on your right and then **bear R** on a lane signposted to St Benet's Benedictine Abbey. There is not much left of the abbey or the windmill that was built in its ruins, but each year a service is held here by the Bishop of Norwich who arrives by boat.

Ride back up the same lane but **turn R** at the T-junction, making straight for Ludham. Then **turn L** at the T-junction. In Ludham you will reach a crossroads by the Kings Arms. Cross over the main road here at the slightly staggered crossroads and, after a

The bridge at Potter Heigham.

couple of hundred yards, **turn R** onto Malthouse Lane.

In just over 1 mile **turn R** at a small crossroads towards Potter Heigham and so back on to the A1062 where you **turn L**. Pass the Falgate Inn and go straight on. Lathams – a famous store which sells almost everything – is on your left, the Museum of the Broads is on your right and the famous Potter Heigham Bridge is dead ahead.

Cyclists can cross this unaccompanied but inexperienced sailors need a Bridge Pilot to get their boats safely under its narrow, low arch. This can be fun to watch.

Return past the Museum but **turn R** onto Station Road and across the A149 into Potter Heigham village. **Turn R** at the T-junction and follow the road round past the particularly beautiful church. **Turn R** at the next T-junction and then **R** again. Cross over a small diagonal crossroads and keep on

the road towards Hickling.

After 2 miles you will reach Hickling. **Turn R** here down Staithe Road to see Hickling Broad. You'll come to the water and you should **turn R** down Hill Common for a few hundred yards to see the thatched boathouses. Return to Staithe Road and **turn R**. This road now becomes Ouse Road.

Turn R at the T-junction and then **L** by the Greyhound pub in Hickling village, towards Stalham. **Turn L** at the junction and, after a mile or so, **turn R** at the crossroads. You will see Sutton church on your left. Take the **second turn L** to Stalham. Ride straight through the village on the main street and the car park is on the far side.

THE BROADS

The Broads may not look man made but they are. They were dug in the Middle Ages at a time when East Anglians had already cut down

the natural forest that covered most of the area. But what remained was a substantial supply of peat which was an efficient, easily available fuel. Monasteries organised the digging – up to a depth of fifteen feet in some places and all done by hand. Consequently the level of the land dropped which meant that it flooded and large shallow lakes were created. This made it necessary to build windpumps to keep the water off the land that was needed for agriculture. The reeds are still harvested for thatching and there is a tradition of wild fowling and fishing here.

Many of the lakes – and rivers such as the Ant and the Thurne – support an area rich in bird and plant life. There are avocets, reeds, sedges, swallowtail butterflies, dragonflies and fish to be seen even though the number of boats and tourists threatens their existence. Conservation measures are helping the Broads to maintain their ecological equilibrium, and there are a great many people who are just happy pottering about on or near water, especially the Norfolk Broads.

(5)

East Dereham and North Elmham

22 miles

This route is right in the heart of Norfolk. Starting from Dereham, which can be busy, especially on market day (Tuesday), you will ride mostly to the north, stopping to admire the amazing workhouse which was built in 1777 and is now the Norfolk Rural Life Museum, and later turning south after visiting the Saxon cathedral remains at North Elmham. The first half of the ride takes you through pasture land, but the second leads you into wider landscapes and brings you back along the course of the River Whitewater which is flowing to join the River Wensum.

This is a gentle ride in which the roads and the views from them are the real pleasures. Not that this is or was a featureless place – far from it. You'll pass through Bilney, named after Thomas Bilney who was burned at the stake for heresy in 1531. Look out for Spreadoak Wood and read the notice on the tree before you consider 'fellinge or carrienge' wood from it.

And if you need a new pair of shoes, this is the ride for you.

Map: OS Landranger 132 North West Norfolk (GR 988134).

Starting point: East Dereham, which is 15 miles west of Norwich on the A47. There are several car parks, none far from the town centre. Some are free.

Dereham can provide you with refreshment at the beginning or end of your ride, but there are other more scenic eating opportunities en route. The Bell at Brisley might be a good choice because it's about halfway and stands on the edge of Brisley's spacious green.

Leave Dereham's main centre by the B1110 towards Fakenham. There's over a mile of built-up area to get past but once you reach the golf club on your left you'll soon come to Quebec Hall on your right.

Turn L here, towards Gressenhall. After about 2 miles **turn R**, signposted to Beetley.

You will come to crossroads in the centre of Gressenhall by the village green and the Swan pub.

Turn R here to Beetley and the Norfolk Rural Life Museum. Ride for about 1½ miles, and the museum is on your left, the Union Farm on your right. This museum gives a detailed and authentic picture of rural life in Norfolk, and even though you will probably not explore it now, you will be impressed by the former Mitford and Launditch Union workhouse in which it is housed. Some 700 people once lived there, and about 150 years ago the weekly cost for each person's food and clothing was 2s 4d.

Return to Gressenhall and cross straight over

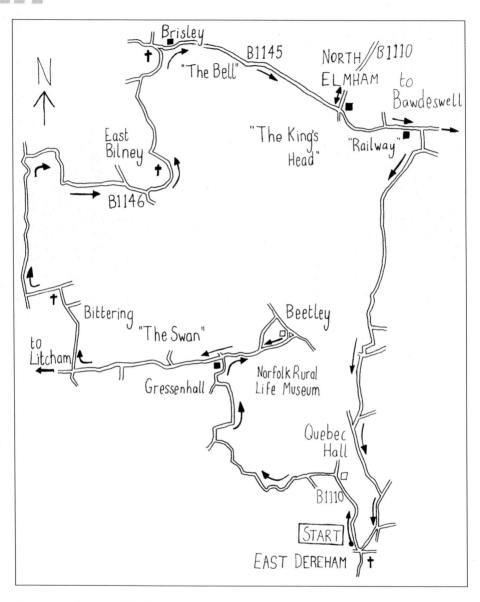

the crossroads, towards Litcham.

After another 2 miles **turn R** towards Bittering and then **L** at the T-junction. Notice the beautiful little church on the left. Its bells are pulled by ropes that hang on the outside.

Turn R at the next T-junction and go straight on for a couple of miles. After a flurry of sharp bends **turn R** towards East Bilney.

This little road leads you to the B1146. **Turn R** on to it, towards Dereham.

The cathedral ruins at North Elmham.

Turn L at the first opportunity, into the lane signposted to the church.

You should pause at both the unusual shoe shop on your right (unusual shoes, unusual shop) and, at the top of the rise, the church on your left.

Follow this lane to the B1145 near Brisley. **Turn R** onto it, and you will see the Bell pub on your left.

After about 3 miles you will reach the crossroads at North Elmham by the King's Head. **Turn L** here and ride up the B1110 for a mile (note the milestone in the wall on your left) and you will come to the ruined Saxon cathedral on your right.

If you go up the B1110 a little further, you will find Elmham Park on your left. This is a vineyard but check opening times if you want to visit.

When you have seen the Saxon site and/or tasted wine, ride back down the way you came as far as the King's Head at the crossroads. **Turn L** here, towards Bawdeswell on the B1145.

After a mile you will come into Worthing. Cross an old railway line and pass the Railway pub on your right.

As you come out of the village **turn R** on the road signposted to Dereham. This road takes you steadily south. On your left is the old railway line, on your right is the River Whitewater, flowing very slowly north.

After about 4 miles **bear R** towards Dereham (don't go to Hoe) and then **L**. This road will take you back to the town centre.

EAST DEREHAM

It is worth exploring the side streets of Dereham and seeking out Bishop Bonner's

An old level crossing.

cottage (right under the town centre church in St Withburga's Lane) with its museum and attractive exterior plaster decoration. Less attractive is the fact that this Bishop sent many Protestants to the burning pyres in the 16th century. There's also a windmill – recently restored with cap, fantail, sails and even an exhibition about windmills – in Cherry Lane.

NORTH ELMHAM

In the 7th century Elmham was chosen as the site of a new see – a cathedral for the religious centre of Norfolk. Three centuries later the see was still important but was moved to Thetford, and then very soon afterwards to Norwich. It was only in 1903 that it was realised that these ruined buildings in North Elmham could be part of the original Saxon cathedral, most of which would have been constructed out of wood. The ruins are actually those of the chapel built for the Bishop when the original cathedral was dismantled or in a state of disrepair. But in 1370 another Bishop found a different use for the chapel. He was keen on hunting and as North Elmham was in good hunting country he converted the chapel into premises to provide living accommodation and he probably also created the moats.

6

Swaffham and Castle Acre

26 miles

This ride starts in the market town of Swaffham, then takes you south into Cockley Cley in the pinewooded and sandy area known as Breckland, and then north to Castle Acre. It is a route studded with evidence of history as ancient as the Cockley Cley site on which there is a reconstruction of an Iceni village and in Castle Acre the remains of a Norman castle and a Cluniac priory. If you are in Swaffham on market day (Saturday) you may be tempted by items of more recent history, for there are a number of bric-à-brac stalls. Treasures from these will weigh down your panniers even though they may uplift your spirits.

On this route you will mostly be riding along straight roads, possibly on routes once favoured by Boudicca, the warrior queen who was reputed to have (but apparently didn't) knives sticking out of her chariot's wheel axles. You won't have to worry about your tyres being slashed, or much traffic at all (whether cars or chariots), so this is a good ride if you like to chat or sing with your companions.

Maps: This route ideally needs three maps – OS Landranger 144 Thetford, Diss, Breckland and Wymondham, 132 North West Norfolk and – for only a very small part of the route which is included in the sketch map – 143 Ely, Wisbech and surrounding area (GR 820085).

Starting point: Swaffham, which is about 25 miles west of Norwich on the A47. Swaffham has several car parks and there is a free lorry park near the centre.

Swaffham has plenty of eating places and Castle Acre, two-thirds of the way round your route, has a good choice of attractive pubs and tea rooms.

This route obliges you to cross – but not to travel along – the busy A47. This should be done with extreme care if you are there at one of the times when there is a lot of traffic. You may feel more in control if you dismount and push your bike across.

Start off from the main town square. Next to the White Hart is Cley Road, a little turning signposted to Cockley Cley. This takes you out of the built-up area onto a straight road lined with pine trees.

After several miles you will reach Cockley Cley where you can cross the road to see the reconstruction of an Iceni village if you

wish. It is designed to show people what life in such a village would have been like sometime around AD 60, at a time when Boudicca had passed through, but before the Romans attacked it. It has a palisade and drawbridge and reed-thatched wooden huts.

Otherwise **turn R** by the Twenty Churchwardens pub, onto the road to

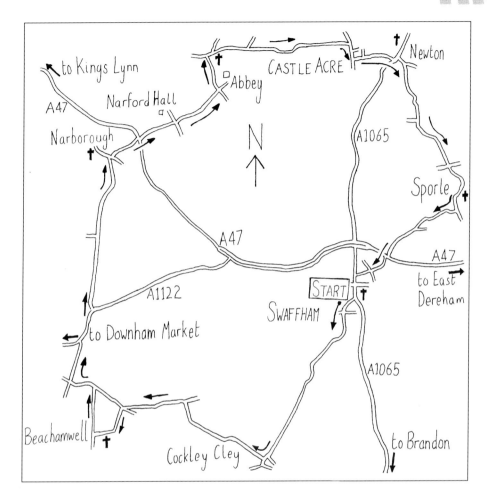

Beachamwell. **Bear L** at the fork.

Turn L at the next T-junction, and **L** again, and then **R** in Beachamwell away from the Great Dane's Head pub. (Note the two representations of a great Dane on the pub sign.)

Pass the exquisite little church on the green here and then **turn R** at the T-junction, towards Fincham. Go round several bends and then **turn L** at the next junction, still heading for Fincham.

At the crossroads **turn R** towards Narborough, and then **R** at the next T-junction onto the A1122 towards Swaffham.

Take the next **L** towards RAF Marham and Narborough. You are riding along the route of the Devil's Dyke, an ancient earthwork built as a defence.

Just keep going steadily for a few miles until you reach Narborough. If you want to explore the rest of the village (where there was once a railway, barge traffic on the river and a turnpike road) take the road to your

Taking a rest at Beachamwell.

left. But otherwise cross almost straight over here, towards Castle Acre and West Acre.

You will reach the A47 and must cross it, very carefully, and take the road that is nearly opposite, towards Castle Acre.

Carry on now, noting Narford Hall in its lovely setting with a lake beyond. Ride straight on. You are parallel with – but cannot see – the River Nar.

Turn L to West Acre and you will pass the remains of an Augustinian priory. **Turn R** at the T-junction towards Castle Acre. Follow along this road for about 3 miles and then **turn R** at the junction and ride down into Castle Acre, noting the road on your left that is signposted to Newton because you will need to return here.

After taking a break for refreshment or sightseeing, return to the road signposted to Newton, and **turn R** onto it. After a mile or so you will reach the A1065. **Turn L** onto it and then **R,** opposite a church.

Go up a slope for half a mile and then **turn R** (there is no signpost).

This is a straight road that crosses two small crossroads en route to Sporle, which is about 4 miles from Newton.

As you come into Sporle note the church on your left and the Squirrels Dray pub. In the middle of the village **turn R** onto the road signposted to Swaffham.

Follow this for a couple of miles until you reach the A47 again. As before be very careful as you cross this busy main road to get onto Sporle Road which is almost immediately opposite and leads back into the centre of Swaffham.

SWAFFHAM

Swaffham is known as the finest Regency town in East Anglia and, although it may not feel elegant now, if you can manage to see the Market Square without traffic you will appreciate the Georgian houses and Assembly Room. There is a magnificent Market Cross and markets are still held on Saturdays. The church and its delicate spire are well worth looking at, and inside you should seek out the story of the Peddlar of Swaffham. Legend has it that he went to London to seek his fortune, but returned home on the advice of a stranger who told him that he would discover treasure beneath a tree on his own land, and he did.

The King's Head, the Greyhound and Horse and Groom are just a few of the pubs where some would say that you can find a different sort of liquid treasure: Norfolk beer.

CASTLE ACRE

There are two major historical features within this village which does not really seem to feel like Norfolk. Much of the castle, which was built on an ancient site at a junction of the Peddars Way and a Roman road, was a Norman manor house. You can also ride under the 11th-century Baileygate, sit in the little village centre and have a meal at either the Ostrich or the Albert Victor. Most of the village is actually the outer bailey of the castle. Then visit the handsome remains of the Cluniac priory, which you can see from the road but must pay to enter. It's worth it.

In the grounds of Narborough Hall.

7

Downham Market and Denver Sluice

14 miles

Downham Market was once a port on the River Ouse but now it hardly feels watery, unlike much of the route which runs alongside wide and mostly man-made waterways that make the area feel more like the Netherlands than Norfolk. The surrounding flat and black land is relieved only by green dykes and, at least in winter, by mini-hills of sugar beet. Still horses graze in a still landscape but the water is moving. The channels you will pass slice through the countryside carrying tonnes of water southwards into Cambridgeshire and as far as Essex.

This ride may take you into an unfamiliar world. Prepare to be surprised.

Map: OS Landranger 143 Ely, Wisbech and surrounding area (GR 611032).

Starting point: Downham Market, which is situated on the A10 about 30 miles north of Cambridge and 10 miles south of King's Lynn. It has several car parks.

Refreshments can be had in Downham Market, but you'll find some riverside pubs too, such as the Jenyns Arms at Denver Sluice, or the Windmill at Ten Mile Bank.

Little of this route is on land that lies much above sea level. It is nearly all on flatlands and fens, between rivers and man-made drainage dykes. Your biggest slopes are probably the bridges. Note that you will need to cross and ride along the A10 on three separate occasions, but only for a total of 2 miles.

Start off from the centre of Downham near the elegant town clock, heading for the A1122 and signs towards Wisbech. Pass the Live and Let Live pub. When you reach the A1122 **turn L** and then, carefully, immediately R towards Denver.

Follow the road down into the village, leaving the church on your left. **Turn sharp R** by the Bell pub, signposted to Denver Windmill. Within a mile you will reach the mill (which was powered by wind until 1941) on your left, standing on the edge of Sluice Common.

Keep riding onwards and over the railway.

Soon you will reach Denver Sluice and an amazing system of channels and rivers controlled by locks and sluices. Make sure that you stop on the bridge to look at it properly and to read the information on the notice board. The map of the waterways is particularly interesting.

Ride over the bridge and past – or into – the Jenyns Arms. Climb up the bank opposite the pub for a close up view of the straight River Delph.

Continue riding along the bank of the River Ouse for several miles. You will pass St Mark's at Ten Mile Bank. A mile further on

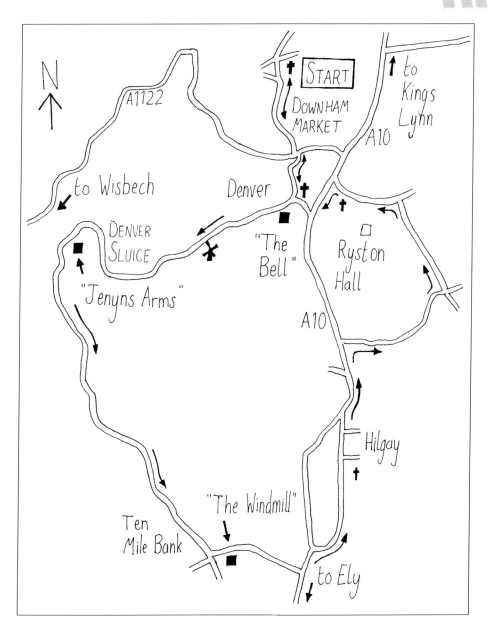

turn L over the bridge and past the Windmill pub.

After another mile you will meet the A10. Turn L onto it and, after a couple of hundred yards, turn R off it towards Hilgay. Ride through Hilgay village and soon after you pass the Rose and Crown turn R, back onto the A10.

A quiet country road.

Stay on it for a mile and then **turn R** towards West Dereham. Just under 2 miles further on **turn L** at a small crossroads towards Denver.

At the small T-junction **turn L** and you will see Ryston Hall on your left, and then its church. Then **turn L** onto the A10 (for the last time) and then **R** into Denver. Follow the road round and you will reach Denver church where you **turn R**.

Take this road back to the A1122, across it and back into Downham Market.

DENVER SLUICE AND THE WATERWAYS

Denver Sluice is the main navigation structure that links the rivers to its south to the tidal waters to its north by controlling their different levels. Old Denver Sluice (the first one) was built in 1651 by Vermuyden. It was attacked by a group of men known as Fen Tigers because it threatened their livelihood of eeling and wildfowling. In 1730 the first navigation lock was built, and this was replaced in 1834. Now Old and New sluices drain the land and allow boats to gain access to all the inland waterways that lie to the south. Steel lock gates control fresh water, salt tides and the river traffic that uses them.

A glance at the map on the sluice bridge reveals unfamiliar, liquid words that define these wet fenlands: residual flow sluice, flood relief cut-off channel. A.G. Wright sluice, Old Bedford River, Ely, Ouse. If you get a puncture, go fishing.

(8)

Wymondham

15 miles

This is an undemanding and peaceful ride. Although it starts and ends in Wymondham, a place easier to pronounce than it appears (just say *Windham*) and even easier to amble around and take refreshment in before setting off or after returning, this route is simply a leisurely cycle through attractive countryside. You'll pass open fields, woodlands, and the watery meadows beside the River Yare. Wymondham has a highly unusual church and you'll pass a handful of small churches, mostly situated away from the heart of the parish to which they belong. Take your time – make this an unhurried expedition.

Map: OS Landranger 144 Thetford & Diss, Breckland and Wymondham (GR 107020).

Starting point: Wymondham, which is just north of the A11 about 6 miles from Attleborough and 8 from Norwich. There are several car parks in the town.

Wymondham has places for coffee and tea as well as several pubs – the Cross Keys in the market place (as much a museum as a pub), the Queen's Head and the Green Dragon. This ride takes you through two villages, each with a pub. For scenic value try the popular pub by the river in Bawburgh, but for no frills yet delicious food try the Bell at Marlingford.

This is one of the shorter rides and has no testing gradients. Just enjoy a steady ride on minor roads.

From wherever you have parked (and there are several places to choose from) look out for signs to Town Green on the northern side of the town. Then look for a sign to Little Melton (B1135) along Melton Road. This leads you to a staggered crossroads where you cross the B1135 and head towards Little Melton and Wramplingham.

Keep on this road (do not take the left turn to Wramplingham) and continue for a few miles until you reach a war memorial. **Turn R** here onto Market Lane. You will soon see

an abandoned and lonely church tower standing next to a very similar one attached to a church.

After a mile or two **turn L** and then, when you reach a T-junction with the B1108, **turn R**.

Take the first **L turn** towards Bawburgh and just before you come into the village over a bridge over the Yare turn L to see the church.

You will find the burial site of St Walstan,

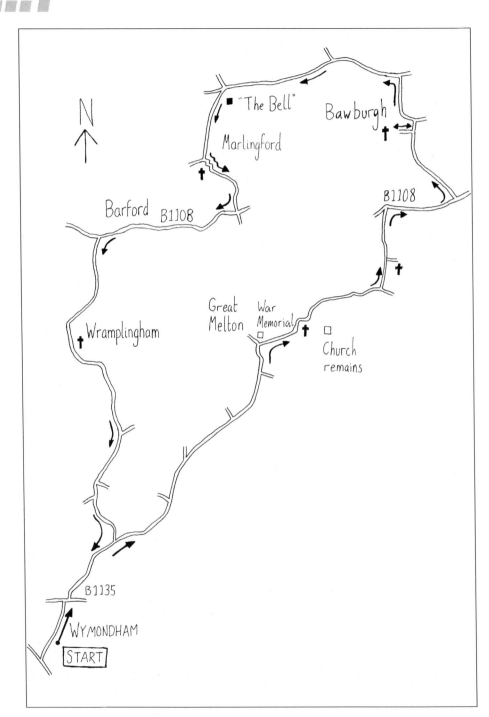

N

"The Bell"

Bawburgh

Marlingford

Barford B1108

B1108

Wramplingham

Great Melton

War Memorial

Church remains

B1135

WYMONDHAM

START

The Green Dragon pub at Wymondham.

patron saint of agriculture and farm workers, and each year there is a special church service followed by a procession down to the nearby St Walstan's Well. Apparently the tradition of drawing and drinking the well water is now no longer recommended!

Go back to the road and **turn L** and there's the pub straight ahead, facing the river. This is a good place for a picnic too.

When you are ready **turn L** here, leaving the pub on your right and the mill on your left.

Turn L at the T-junction towards Marlingford and continue riding along the course of the Yare. When you come into Marlingford **turn L** by the Bell. **Turn L** at the next T-junction and cross the river again.

Turn R at the crossroads onto the B1108 towards Barford and then, after 2 miles, **turn L** along The Street towards Wramplingham and Wymondham. Follow along here through Wramplingham, past a collection of fine, large houses and out past the church which is on your left.

After about 3 miles you will reach a junction. **Turn R** here and you will reach the staggered crossroads you crossed on your outward journey. Go straight over and into Wymondham, down towards Town Green and your starting point.

WYMONDHAM

This little town on the River Tiffey has its roots in history. In the centre is a timber-framed, octagonal market cross. This has been there since 1618 but it replaces an earlier one that was burned down. In 1107 Wymondham Abbey was built by the Benedictines, the most powerful and influential religious order of the Middle Ages. Unfortunately, the local people did not like the Benedictines and even the Pope became involved in trying to resolve local conflicts. He failed and a wall was built across the church dividing it into two parts, each with its own tower. As each side rang its own bells for its own congregations it must have been confusing as well as noisy for those who lived nearby. Later much of the abbey was destroyed, but today you can see the church still with its two towers (one of which housed the gallows for Robert Kett, a leader of the revolt against enclosure in the 16th century) and some of the abbey ruins, all set in a spacious area containing graves and pine trees.

9

Thetford and Boudicca's territory

22 miles

All of the roads in this ride go through Breckland, the sandy, wooded heath that covers parts of Suffolk and Norfolk. It was crossed first by the Iceni, a tribe led by Boudicca, and then by the Romans and later still by the Danes. Now it's your turn. Much of your route is along straight roads but you'll enjoy seeing little bridges and watery meadows. East Harling is a small town with a special, quiet character, but you should spend at least half an hour off your bike in Thetford to explore the watermill and the flinty remains of the priory and see the statue of Thomas Paine, rebellious author of *The Rights of Man*.

Other features of the ride are glimpses of the school attended by Princess Diana, forests, the stately Euston Hall and a beautiful country park in which to stretch your legs at the end of your ride.

Map: OS Landranger 144 Thetford & Diss, Breckland & Wymondham (GR 956806).

Starting point: Knettishall Heath Country Park. This park is situated a mile or two south of the A1066 and about 10 miles east of Thetford, near the village of Garboldisham. There is plenty of room for cars, but make sure that you find the main country park. This route has fewer opportunities for refreshments so I would suggest taking a picnic with you.

Much of this ride takes you along the courses – not necessarily always very close – of two rivers, the Thet and the Little Ouse. This means that it's flat and straight, and, because the Little Ouse is the boundary between Norfolk and Suffolk, you will ride in two counties.

Face the road by the entrance to the park and **turn R** (ie not over the small road that goes over the bridge), and then **L**. Ride for a couple of miles, noticing the large house on the other side of the river, to your left. This is Riddlesworth Hall, where Diana, Princess of Wales went to school.

When you reach the crossroads look up to your right. Notice the church which has been made into a house. Turn L here and over the Little Ouse, through Gasthorpe and

straight across the A1066. You are on a Roman road which takes you through woodland.

At the next road junction **bear L** onto the B1111 and ride on into East Harling. It is worth pausing in the attractive square of this little town before moving on. You'll pass the Swan Inn – but once East Harling had 13 inns or ale houses. Stay on the main road which bears left.

A converted church near Knettishall.

You will find Harling Vineyards on your right, set in the grounds of a Victorian Gothic mansion and worth calling in for a wine tasting – but check opening times.

Then pass the particularly lovely church with its elegant spire, also on your right, before **turning L** at the next turn, signposted to Bridgham.

You will reach Bridgham after a straight ride of a couple of miles. Once through the village **turn L** down a small road for a breather by a pretty bridge. Then **return** to the road you were on and **turn L**, continuing in the direction you were travelling in.

Then ride on to Brettenham. **Turn L** here to see a beautiful church in a lovely open setting. Then **return** to the road you were on and continue to Kilverstone. Soon after Kilverstone you meet the A1075. **Turn L** onto it and ride down into Thetford, a good

place for a break and a wander around between historic buildings made of flint.

When you leave Thetford take the A1088. Although a main road it is not too busy. Stay on it for 3 miles until you reach Euston, where you **turn L** towards Rushford.

However, if you want to visit Euston Hall, stay on the main road for another few hundred yards. Euston Hall is famous both for the art collection it houses and also for the fact that it is supposed to be the first big country house to be supplied, in the 17th century, with running water. If the house is closed you'll still be able to visit the church.

When you have been to the Hall return along the A1088 to take the **R turn** to Rushford.

The road to Rushford runs through a belt of woodland. **Turn R** at Rushford and then a few hundred yards further on **take the L**

A peaceful scene at Bridgham.

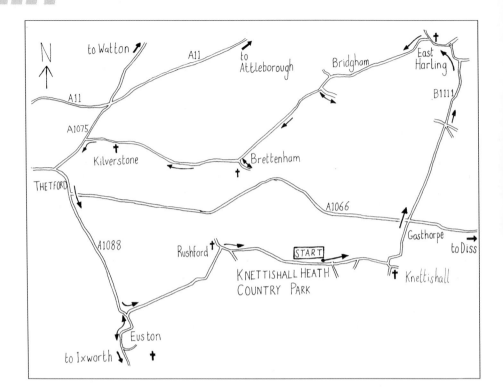

fork at the junction towards Knettishall. This will bring you back to your starting point at the country park.

THETFORD
Around 1,000 years ago Thetford was the capital of East Anglia. Evidence of its economic, social and religious power can be seen in the remains of its castle mounds and three priories. The Nuns' Bridges that cross both the River Thet and the Little Ouse were built at the places where people used to ford the rivers – especially those travelling along the Icknield Way, the Neolithic route that ran from Salisbury Plain to the Wash. A few minutes' wander around Thetford looking at the

buildings will demonstrate the importance of flint, which was first mined at the nearby Grimes Graves 4,000 years ago by men using deer antlers. Thetford also had its own mint for two centuries.

KNETTISHALL HEATH COUNTRY PARK
This is a riverside park in Breckland where three long distance pathways meet: the ancient Peddars Way, the Icknield Way and the new Angles Way. Peddars Way was a straight Celtic track, later adopted and metalled by the Romans, that started near Thetford and ran north to the coast, but now Knettishall Heath is its official southern end. Enjoy relaxing here after your ride. Even a short stroll may reveal some of the park's rich wildlife.

10

Halesworth and Laxfield

20 miles

The features of this route do not shout out and demand attention. They are simply the pleasures that any ride in lovely countryside provides: soft landscapes, little lanes, real pubs, timbered houses, rows of vegetables in gardens. Even the stately home you'll pass is just there, standing back from the road without any advertisement or razzmatazz. There's a general feeling of an absence of energy but this is positive and to be enjoyed just as it might be in a quiet village on the continent. If seeking perfection, do this ride on a warm, calm day when you can just amble along at your own pace.

Map: OS Landranger 156 Saxmundham and Aldeburgh (GR 387777).

Starting point: Halesworth, on the A144, about 15 miles south-west of Lowestoft. Its main car park is in the centre of town just off the main road, but you may be able to find other places too.

The main street of Halesworth is for pedestrians only and you can certainly find tea and coffee places here to set you up for the ride. But save most of your appetite for Laxfield where there is a special pub.

There are a few ups and downs on this route – but they serve to make you feel that you deserve that extra large helping of chocolate cake. Follow the directions carefully, for this ride takes you on some really small lanes.

With the car park behind you come out onto the A144, and **turn R** towards Ipswich. You will need to cross (carefully) over a roundabout and keep on the main road, signposted towards Saxmundham and Ipswich, for a mile until you are out of the town.

When the main road to Ipswich turns sharply to the left do not follow it but keep going **straight on**, onto the B1117 towards Walpole. You will soon leave the built-up area.

Ride along here for a little over a mile, and

turn R (staying on the B1117) when you reach a T-junction. Soon you will come into Walpole where you need to **turn L** onto a minor road signposted to Peasenhall.

Then just keep riding for about 4 miles along between fields and woods, until you reach Sibton, where you **turn L** by the White Horse, and then ride on and over the bridge and then **R** into Peasenhall. At the A1120 note Weavers on your left as you **turn R** onto the main road. It is an excellent place for your lunch or coffee stop. The village has some beautiful houses but there is no pub.

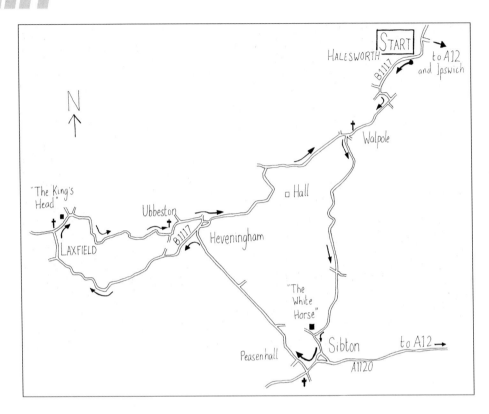

At the main crossroads in Peasenhall **turn R** towards Laxfield and Heveningham. Ride down a steepish hill and then along this former Roman road for several miles until you reach a T-junction. **Turn L** here onto the B1117.

Carry on through Ubbeston Green and continue until you reach the village of Laxfield. You'll enter the village opposite the church. **Turn R** here and after a couple of hundred yards you will see the King's Head, also known as the Low House, down a lane to your left. Make sure you have a look in here even if you don't have a drink and lunch.

When you are ready, **turn L** onto the road you were on before, but now you are going out of Laxfield. **Turn R** at a small crossroads

and follow a winding lane towards Ubbeston. After a couple of miles you will see the church on your left. Keep on the same road as far as Heveningham.

Turn R and immediately **L** into Heveningham and then **L** onto the B1117. After a while you will see the magnificent Heveningham Hall on your right. The gardens of this Palladian stately home were designed by Capability Brown.

Carry on into Walpole and straight through on the same road and route which you were riding along earlier today in the opposite direction.

After a mile or so **turn L**, still on the B1117, towards Halesworth which is about 2 miles away.

HALESWORTH

This small town is on the River Blythe and it was the transport along this river that contributed to the success of Halesworth's breweries in the 18th century. Nowadays, although the Blythe still passes through on its way to Blythburgh and the coast, the town remains a pleasant, unspoiled place. There's a small museum that opens in the summer, but Halesworth can be enjoyed just for what it is – a Suffolk community whose history is patently visible in its buildings.

LAXFIELD

Nowadays Laxfield's claim to fame rests largely on the Low House pub. The sign shows a king's head, and indeed the pub's official name is the King's Head, but whatever it's called it's a special place. The interior consists of a series of interconnected and unrestored rooms with simple benches and central tables, and a tap room at the back. Don't look for the bar because you won't find one, but enjoy the welcome and rare proper pub-ness with no frills. Because people value this you may find that many weekend customers include teams of clog dancers, people who've arrived by horse and carriage, and fellow cyclists.

Opposite the church, in the Guildhall, is a small museum of Suffolk village life showing reconstructions of domestic and workshop environments.

(11)
Southwold and Covehithe
13 miles

This, a shorter route than most in this book, is a leisurely ride that takes you almost as far east as you can get in England. Southwold is perfect for anyone who prefers proper old-fashioned beaches with shingle and beach huts, to big crowds and noisy entertainment – and for anyone who enjoys real ale. If you like both beaches and beer you'll love it here. Southwold is as famous for its Adnams Brewery – with its splendid malty smell – as for its distinctive white lighthouse.

This is the only ride on which a walk is compulsory. The view from the cliffs at Covehithe is magnificent and can of course be enjoyed by just being looked at. But I recommend that you leave your bike and take a half hour walk along the Suffolk Coastal Path to breathe in sea air, watch sea birds and count ships on the horizon.

Map: OS Landranger 156 Saxmundham and Aldeburgh (GR 513769).

Starting point: Southwold, which is on the A1095 about 12 miles south of Lowestoft on the east coast. Start from the car park at Sole Bay. This is right on the coast north of Southwold and you will find it if you turn left at the Pier Avenue hotel as you enter the town. It may be full in summer, and you may need to seek a parking place elsewhere.

Southwold is full of buildings and shops that will stimulate your interest and appetite and may well delay your start. But as it's not a long ride you'll be back here in plenty of time to enjoy them later on. There are no refreshments at Covehithe so it may be worth taking a snack or picnic to enjoy on the cliffs or down on the beach.

This route does not take you more than a few miles inland, and you'll be able to smell the sea as you ride.

Ride from Sole Bay along the front into the centre of Southwold. After a meander around the town to guarantee that you resolve to explore it on your return, set off on the A1095 – the only main road.

After a mile take the first **R turn** onto the B1127 towards Wrentham. Keep going for about 2 miles until you reach a turning to

your left towards Cove Bottom. **Turn L** here and ride on until you rejoin the B1127 at South Cove. **Turn L** here and you will see the little church on your right.

Carry on to Wrentham where you should beware of the A12. You might want to call in at the small art gallery (near the shop on your right) or pause here before taking the

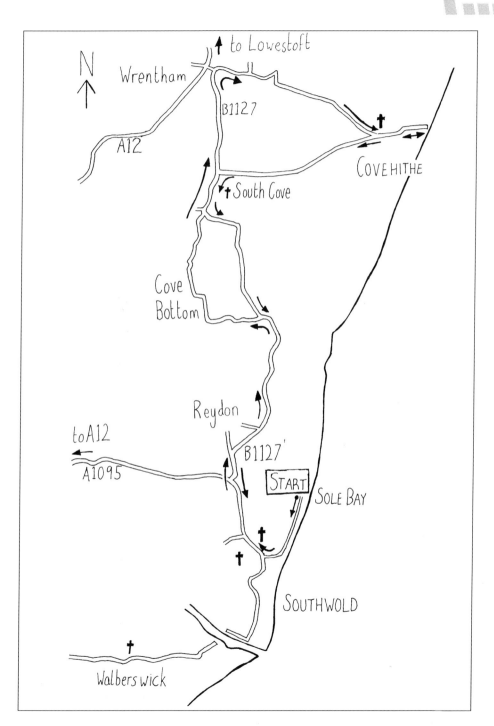

On the open road.

minor road which is signposted to Covehithe and is almost directly opposite the road on which you approached, in the centre of the village.

Now ride for a little over 2 miles. You are going straight towards the sea and will see Covehithe's special churches ahead on your left before you reach them. These are well worth stopping at. Then ride on, getting off your bike to pass the barrier marked 'Danger' or leaving it by the roadside. After walking for a few yards you will find yourself literally on the cliff's edge.

Take in the amazing view and go for an outstanding cliff top walk in either direction, along the Suffolk Coastal Path. If you go to the left you can get down onto the beach and see the bright, brittle orange sand from the cliff that is gradually crumbling away, inch by inch.

Once on your bike again ride back the way

you came, but **turn L** to Southwold when the road forks just past Covehithe church. Then ride for a couple of miles and over a minor crossroads and on until you meet the B1127. **Turn L** here and continue through South Cove and stay on the same road. After a few miles you will come to Reydon Business Park. **Turn L** in Reydon and then **L** at the A1095.

You will soon be back in Southwold. **Turn L** by the Pier Avenue hotel if you want to return to the Sole Bay car park.

But if you still have energy, carry on into the centre and, when the A1095 ceases to exist, **bear R** and find the lane that leads to Walberswick. It's a lovely ride past the dunes but in summer you will find a special bonus when you reach the wide River Blythe: a ferryboat for pedestrians – and their bikes – which will allow you to cross the river and have a spin around Walberswick.

SOUTHWOLD

Southwold is the most elegant of East Anglian seaside resorts, despite early wars and calamities. Most of the original town was destroyed by a fire in 1659 and this led to several greens being created to prevent any future fire from spreading rapidly. Fort Green and Gun Green sound warlike but today they are gentle and peaceful focal points of Southwold. The Sole Bay Inn is named after a violent and inconclusive battle fought against the Dutch in nearby Sole Bay, but the bay and the open sea were also the source of Southwold's other income – fish. Fish and chips with Adnams beer is probably the perfect meal here.

COVEHITHE

Once Covehithe was an established village and port with enough people to fill a large parish church. But coastal erosion here means that the land literally falls away – between two and three metres crumble away each year as a result of the sea's action. As the land was lost the population decreased, so much so that in the 18th century the villagers built a new, small church more suited to their needs. They built it within the site of the original one, using its stones and building materials and finishing it off with a thatched roof.

(12)

Eye, Hoxne and Wingfield

25 miles

This ride straddles the Waveney valley and the border between Norfolk and Suffolk. It takes you through quiet, undulating countryside and past some spectacular buildings. Starting from Eye, a delightful little market town whose soaring 100 foot church tower advertises its former importance, you will make for Hoxne, the village in which it is thought that the King of East Anglia was killed by the Danes and where an amazing Roman hoard of treasure was recently unearthed. You will ride on to Wingfield and then north across the River Waveney and alongside an airfield used by the USA 100th Bomber Group in World War II. It is easy to imagine how airmen returning from dangerous missions in Germany must have felt as they recognised the windmill at Billingford and came in to land safely amongst peaceful lanes, gentle woodlands and soft fields.

Map: OS Landranger 156 Saxmundham and Aldeburgh (GR 145738).

Starting point: Eye car park, between Buckshorn Lane and Church Street, in Eye, just east of the A140 about 20 miles south-west of Norwich.

Eye has plenty of places to eat and buy provisions to take with you, although there are en route opportunities to stop at pubs, such as the De La Pole Arms at Wingfield or the Greyhound at Brockdish, which are respectively just before and just beyond halfway.

This route is not strenuous – enjoy it.

Come out of the car park onto Church Street and **turn R**. Ride straight down. The castle is up on your right, the imposing church on your left.

Bear L at the road junction towards Stradbroke. This is the B1117.

Cross over the River Dove at Abbey Bridge and continue for a mile or so until you reach Burnt House Farm. **Turn L** at the crossroads here, towards Hoxne and Scole.

Follow the road through open fields, ignoring the turn to Hoxne Cross Street, and continue straight down into Hoxne village. This has a traditional village main street with the Swan pub. Ride along the street and up to the top, then **turn R** onto the B1118, and then almost immediately **L** to the church.

The church has a simple display about Hoxne but is particularly informative about the gleaming hoard of silver, gold and coins found locally in 1992.

Come out of the church drive, **turn R** and **then L** back into Hoxne's main street where you came from.

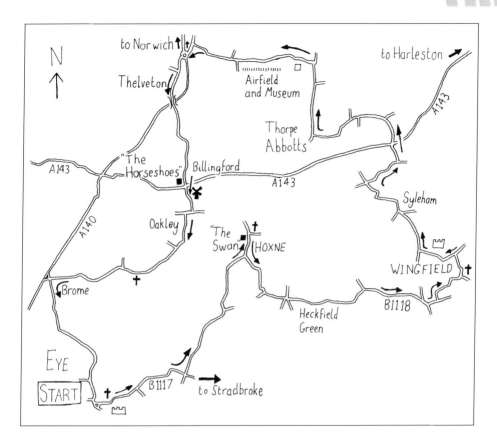

Bear L where the road forks and ride over Goldbrook Bridge, past St Edmunds Hall with its inscription stating that King Edmund was slain nearby.

Cross over the crossroads at Heckfield Green (a name connected with the hemp industry that flourished from the 16th to the 19th century) and on until you meet the B1118. **Turn R** here and then, after a couple of miles, **take the second L turn** towards Wingfield Street.

After a few hundred yards **turn L** into a small lane. Follow this into Wingfield, where you will see the 18th-century Old College facing you. This marvellous building, built by Sir John Wingfield, is made of timbers which have been plastered over on the outside but are exposed on the interior. Exhibitions and concerts are held here and there are extensive gardens, with moats and a topiary.

Turn L and you will find the De La Pole Arms on the left and the church – with memorials and effigies inside of De La Poles and Wingfields – on your right.

Ride on until the T-junction, where you should **turn L**. The road takes you across a wide, meadowy common where cattle and horses are tethered. Keep a look out on the right for Wingfield Castle and its moat, hidden behind the trees and worth stopping for.

Billingford Mill.

Turn **R** at the T-junction. This road is signposted towards Hoxne, but after a mile or so ignore the left turn to Hoxne and stay on your road towards Brockdish.

Turn **R** at the next T-junction, unless you want to explore the lane opposite which will take you to Syleham's round towered church in its green setting.

Continue on to Syleham House and **turn L** down Grove Road. You will pass the pond, ride over the bridge across the River Waveney and into Norfolk, and then go under the A143.

Before you **bear L** towards Thorpe Abbotts you might want to take advantage of the Greyhound, just up to your right on the north side of the A143.

The road takes you on a wide curve for a couple of miles. You will pass an impressive house, The Grange, on your left.

When you reach the covered pump at Thorpe Abbotts **turn R** along Mill Street towards Dickleburgh. Ride along here and **turn L** at the first (unsignposted) turning. This road is the boundary of the former Thorpe Abbotts airfield.

This is privately owned land but within half a mile you will reach, on your left, the airfield's interesting museum.

Continue on into Dickleburgh and **turn L** when you reach a T-junction. Carry on until you come to a roundabout on the A140. This can be busy, but cross straight over towards Thelveton.

After a mile you will cross the A140 again, this time on a flyover. Then the road enters rural territory again and you have a peaceful route to Billingford. You will be able to see its splendid windmill as you approach.

Cross the main road at the Horseshoes, and then a little bridge over the River Waveney and back into Suffolk.

At the next junction **turn R** and then, in the village of Oakley, **turn L**.

Follow this road towards Brome, passing Oakley House, then the entrance to Brome Hall and Brome church. At the crossroads **turn L** towards Eye.

After about 3 miles you will enter Eye. Note the Bedingfield Almshouses on the left, built in 1636 for four widows, and then Linden House, set back from the road on the left.

Keep L at the Town Hall and then **turn L** into Church Street. The car park from which you set off is on the right.

EYE
The name Eye originates from the Saxon word for island, but there is little evidence today of the marshes and rivers that nearly surrounded the town hundreds of years ago. Parts of Eye Castle are still standing on Castle Hill above the town which is full of historic interest: a church which was started in the 13th century and is famous for its magnificent tower, a Guildhall, one of the tiniest theatres in England, a crinkle crankle wall and many distinctive and attractive houses and streets.

Once Eye had nearly a thousand more inhabitants than it has today. Industries included brewing, iron foundries and flax making. A grammar school was needed and there was a market as early as 1066. Make sure that before you set off for the ride or when you return you wander around, enjoy the relaxed atmosphere and are aware of the past.

HOXNE
Hoxne was once more important than Eye, but now it seems to be a perfect example of a typical quiet and lovely Suffolk village. It is

thought, however, that near here Edmund, crowned King of the East Angles in AD 855, was killed by the arrows of Danes because he refused to agree to their terms of peace or to renounce his Christian faith.

Don't let this unhappy fact prevent you from admiring the village and its church, or from marvelling at the thought of the Hoxne treasure. This consists of nearly 15,000 coins and 200 gold and silver items discovered on a local farm in 1992 by someone with a metal detector searching for a lost hammer. But you will have to go to the British Museum to see the find.

THORPE ABBOTTS AIRFIELD

This home of the 100th Bomber Group and their Flying Fortress bombers was constructed in 1942. The first of over 300 missions took place in 1943, but heavy losses meant that the group was gruesomely nicknamed 'The Bloody Hundredth'. The control tower has been restored and houses a memorial as well as a fascinating museum of equipment and memorabilia. Two Nissen huts and small sections of runways still remain. Around 3,000 US airmen were stationed here in the Second World War, mostly accommodated in camps within the nearby woods – a fact that must have had significant impact on the local community.

Wingfield Old College.

13
Newmarket, Exning and Wicken Fen
26 miles

This route wanders through and round the small bulge of Suffolk that sticks improbably into Cambridgeshire and contains Newmarket – the heart of English horse-racing. Every visitor is bound to see evidence of this: betting shops, paddocks, stables and – best of all – racehorses and their riders trotting along the road on their way to or from the training gallops.

Once in fenland you will find a completely different atmosphere as you ride under immense skies and through acres of flat fields of black earth scored with dykes, including the famous Devil's Dyke. The age, simplicity and remoteness of this watery place make it difficult to remember that the elegance and excitement of Newmarket and Cambridge are less than 10 miles away. Instead of horses, perhaps you'll see herons, ducks and swans.

Map: OS Landranger 154 Cambridge and Newmarket (GR 645635).

Starting point: Newmarket, which is about 15 miles east of Cambridge. It is easily reached from the A14, which runs a little to its north. The town has several car parks, and the long stay one is free.

Newmarket has plenty of eating places, but I would recommend a picnic lunch by the river or a visit to the Five Miles From Anywhere No Hurry pub, even though you reach both of these before the halfway mark.

You will hardly need your gears on account of hills for once you are out of Newmarket there aren't any – but you may need them to deal with wind.

Note: This is the one ride in the book that is not recommended to those with children or to anyone who is not a confident cyclist. This is because the second half of the route includes a stretch of main road.

Go to where the main A1304 (the High Street running through Newmarket) meets the A142 signposted towards Exning. After 2 miles **turn L** at the roundabout and follow a minor road.

This takes you past studs where you can see valuable horses looking over their expensive stable doors, and get a taste of what makes much of Newmarket tick. Follow the road round to the right and up a hill.

Turn R when you will meet Exning Road. You will ride under the A14 and arrive in Exning. Pass the church (on your left) and then **turn L** at the White Horse. Go along Swan Lane and past the White Swan and Jolly Butchers.

Then **turn L** onto Burwell Road, the B1103.

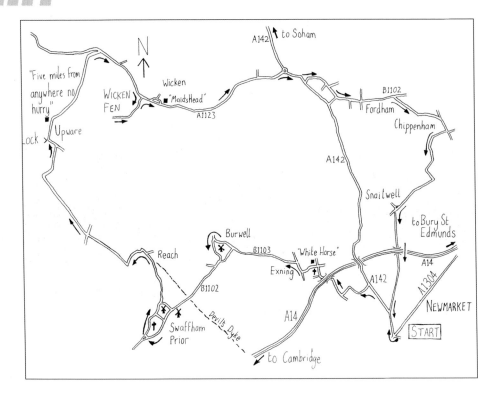

You will pass modern houses and see a one-sailed windmill on your left and the thatched base of a windmill on your right – the first of many mills you will see. Do not turn left towards Swaffham Prior.

Turn L at the road junction and then **L** again, where you will see signs (to the left) to the museum which is next door to the mill that overlooks a small housing estate. When you go back from the mill to the road the church is on the right-hand side. A particularly poignant memorial in the churchyard commemorates 73 people who died in 1727 while watching a play in a thatched barn which caught fire. The doors had been locked to prevent people entering after the play had begun.

Continue past the church and keep on the B1102 towards Swaffham Prior. A mile or so later you will cross the Devil's Dyke, a remarkable earthwork built in the Bronze Age to defend East Anglia.

You will see two windmills ahead of you, one on each side of the road. Soon after passing them **turn R** towards Swaffham Prior. Then **turn R** towards Reach and after a mile or two you will come to Reach's village green and the King's Head Dyke's End pub.

Turn L on the road signposted Upware, along Great Lane, and continue through the village, following the road to Upware.

You are now in the fens. When you reach a slightly staggered crossroads cross over, although there is no signpost. This is flat country of fine black earth.

Upware Lock.

Ride for a few miles, following the road sharply to the right and then **turn L** at the T-junction. Keep going up a rise and you will reach Upware Lock. It's worth stopping here to look at the swans and narrow boats, and a boat may pass through the lock if you're lucky.

Continue down for about half a mile and **turn sharp L** where the road bends. This lane takes you to the brilliantly named and positioned Five Miles From Anywhere No Hurry pub which has a garden leading down the River Cam.

Then ride back up the lane away from the pub and onwards, not back the way you came.

You will then reach the main A1123, which is not usually busy but can carry heavy traffic. **Turn R** onto it and ride into Wicken. Wicken Fen is signposted to your right, and if you have decided to take time

to visit it, this is where you turn off. Once back on the A1123 (if you left it) carry on, passing the Maid's Head on your left, and ride for several miles to the roundabout with the A142. This is a big junction and you need to **turn R**. You might feel safer to get off and push your bike across the roads as if you were a pedestrian. Once on the A142 ride (or walk) for half a mile and **turn L** at the first turning, just before the sign for Fordham. Cross over the first crossroads and follow the road through the village to the left and on to the B1102.

Continue for a mile and **turn R** towards Chippenham. At the junction continue into Chippenham and then **turn R** towards Snailwell. **Turn L** at the crossroads in Snailwell and ride down under the A14 and back into Newmarket.

NEWMARKET
Newmarket is dominated by horse-racing. Even

The attractive garden of the Five Miles From Anywhere No Hurry pub.

if you are not interested in racing it's difficult to ignore the horses that you'll ride past along the roads and the ones you'll see being exercised. If you can get to the heath in the early morning you'll find hundreds of.stable lads taking the horses out for training. This is a place where money changes hands fast, and where the performance of horses and riders is always under discussion even though the owners of the horses may visit only rarely. Your bike may excite your interest and even affection, but horses in Newmarket are the subjects of real passion.

DEVIL'S DYKE

This impressive earthwork consists of a bank and ditch up to 100 feet wide that extends more than 10 miles. It was probably built because the nearby Icknield Way meant that invaders could easily reach the heart of East Anglia, so a defence was needed. It is now a Site of Special Scientific Interest and has unusual wild flowers and butterflies. The Dyke ends at the little village of Reach, where at the fair held each May the Mayor of Cambridge throws coins for children who scramble to be lucky.

(14)

Woolpit and Walsham-le-Willows

24 miles

This route through mid-Suffolk takes you in and out of villages that were once the economic backbone of rural life. Now few people here make their living from the surrounding land, for today hundreds of acres can be managed by a handful of vast machines that do the work of teams of horses and horsemen. But reminders of other former sources of power are still visible in the shape of wind and watermills, and although the grinding of grain that these used to do can now be done faster and more cheaply by modern technology, some are still in working order. If you go up close to Pakenham mill when its sails are turning you will not fail to be impressed by the sheer size and the noise.

Woolpit and Walsham-le-Willows are places to pause in, and if you only visit one church, make it Woolpit. Its distinctive and decorated spire stands above a vast church that dwarfs the little village square.

Map: OS Landranger 155 Bury St Edmunds, Sudbury and Stowmarket (GR 975625).

Starting point: Woolpit. This is about 20 miles north-west of Ipswich, just off the A14. There is no car park here, but parking on the street will not be a problem.

Elm House Gallery can provide a cup of coffee to start you off, and you should visit the church either now or at the end of your ride.

This ride is gentle – you won't struggle for more than a few minutes at a time, and if it feels like a struggle you can just give in, get off and push.

Start from the church. Facing this **set off to the L**, into the centre and leaving the little covered well on your right. Follow the road and **turn R** when you reach the Plough.

At the T-junction **turn R** and cycle towards Drinkstone. Your first (not-working) windmill is up to the right of the road.

Dip down and up in Drinkstone, staying on the same road, and **turn R** at the first (small) crossroads. Follow this lane down and over the A14. **Turn L** at the T-junction and then **R**.

After less than a mile **turn L** and then, after a few hundred yards, **turn R**. Follow this road over the railway line and as far as a fork by a pub. **Turn L** here and ride into Thurston.

Turn R at the crossroads towards Pakenham, leaving the church on your right. Go over the crossroads.

After nearly 2 miles you will pass Pakenham church on your right. Immediately after this **turn L** past a pub and ride through Pakenham.

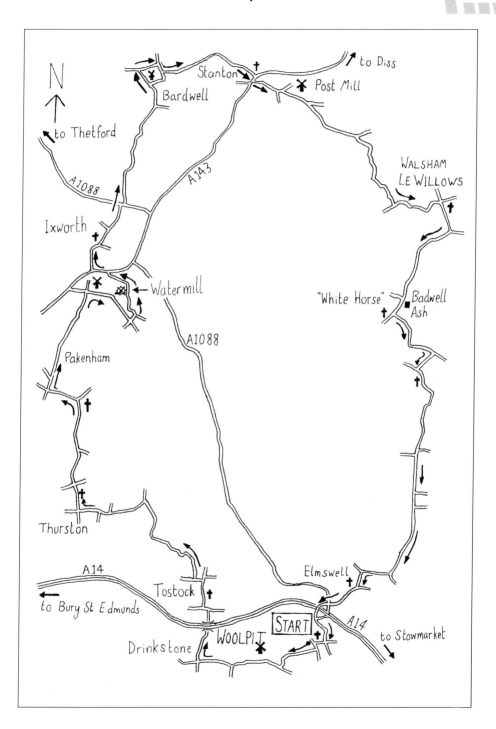

Some of the residents taking a walk.

Turn R at the crossroads and ride along a former Roman road until you reach a windmill. **Turn R** just before it and then, after a mile, **turn L** at the T-junction. **Turn L** again and you will find Pakenham watermill.

Continue to the A143 and **turn L** onto this busy road. You only need to be on it for a few hundred yards, but be careful. When you reach the crossroads **turn R** into Ixworth where there are two pubs, the Pykkerell and the Greyhound.

Ride straight up the High Street. The church is on your left. Soon after the fire station you meet the A1088. Cross (almost) straight over towards Bardwell.

You will pass Bardwell Manor, and then come into Bardwell past its church. **Turn R** at the T-junction and go past the old windmill. **Turn R** at the next T-junction towards Stanton, past the Six Bells pub.

Ride into Stanton, crossing straight over the A143 again and into the village. Stanton post mill stands on your left. **Bear R** at the fork towards Walsham-le-Willows. After nearly 3 miles you will reach a T-junction. **Turn L** here and you will come into Walsham at a crossroads.

It is worth exploring here for a while before taking the road from the crossroads (towards the right from the direction you came) towards Badwell Ash. You should leave the church on your left.

Turn R at the next T-junction and ride for over 2 miles into Badwell Ash. The White Horse pub and the church are on your right. **Turn L** opposite the church, and then **R** after a mile.

At the T-junction **turn L** into Great Ashfield and ride along a straight road for several miles towards Elmswell. Cross over the level crossing and then **turn R**. Follow this road

A shady tree can be welcome on a hot day.

and **turn R** by the Almshouses, (note their sundial), and the church, both on your right.

You will ride down to a roundabout. Cross straight over towards Woolpit and the road will take you up and over the A14. At the crossroads **turn R** into Woolpit and back to where you started.

WOOLPIT

It is thought that the name Woolpit may refer to a pit where wolves lived, but Woolpit's most famous legend is that of the Green Children. Apparently some peasants found two children with green skin (note the village sign) appearing from a cavern in the ground. These children only ate green food and they described a country where everything was green. The story says that the boy pined and died while the girl grew up and married.

Today you can enjoy a drink in the Swan which was built when Shakespeare was alive, sit down in the tea room, visit the museum and the spectacular church with its elegant tower and hammerbeam roof. It is hard to imagine that in the 1640s this church was ransacked by Puritan zealots who wrecked paintings, windows and ornaments.

WALSHAM-LE-WILLOWS

Although named for its willow trees, Walsham's stream is probably its most noticeable feature today. This runs down the main street which is lined with an attractive hotch potch of houses,

some of brick, some of weatherboard. One of the old pubs, the Blue Boar, was used as the Petty Sessions for the Hiring and Retaining of Servants in the late 17th and 18th centuries. An Act of Parliament obliged landowners to employ workers on a yearly contract rather than a daily one and in today's climate of staff cutbacks it is not hard to imagine how stressful it must have been for keen horsemen and farmworkers waiting and hoping for employment that would guarantee them and their families a wage for a year.

In 1911 there was an incident at the annual Ancient Order of Foresters Gala – probably rather like a village fete – which led to armed warfare between the locals and a visiting fair, resulting in the accidental shooting of a passer-by.

WATERMILLS AND WINDMILLS

In the 18th and 19th centuries every rural community needed a mill to grind wheat into flour. This need was as basic as our need to have a shop or well-stocked freezer within reach. Many of these mills went on working until after the Second World War, but the ones that still work usually do so as the result of a few enthusiastic individuals who are determined not to let this important part of the rural heritage fall into disrepair. On this ride you will see one watermill which is well worth stopping for, and windmills in states that vary from sail-less to excellent working order. Look out too for names like Mill Lane or Mill House that may be reminders of other mills.

15

Framlingham, Saxtead Mill and Wickham Market

18 miles

The starting point of this ride – Framlingham Castle – is wonderfully romantic. It is an outstanding story book castle within a now dry moat, and it has a house inside. Just a few miles from the castle is Saxtead Green Post Mill which is worth getting right up close to even if you happen to visit it on a day when it is not open. But if you witness the sails turning you may want to stay longer than you thought.

This is a route through unadvertised and therefore unspoiled Suffolk: the real thing! Go to enjoy the fields, the woods, the brick and flint farm buildings, the gardens of ordinary houses. Easton is a delightful village whose church, pub and special wall may cause you to slow down. Wickham Market's little square with its tempting tea room and patio may cause you to stop completely.

Map: OS Landranger 156 Saxmundham and Aldeburgh (GR 296638).

Starting point: Framlingham, which is on the B1116, about 14 miles north of Ipswich. Parking is available at the castle, but check the closing time of this car park. There are other places to park in Framlingham.

Wickham Market is mid route and has places for refreshment, but the White Horse in Easton might be a good place for lunch.

Part of this route lies along the course of the infant River Deben, which means that there are some slight descents and ascents.

Stand with your back to Framlingham Castle and head off **to the R**, towards the main square. **Turn R** here and ride down the sloping square and out to a junction where you **turn R** onto the B1119 towards Stowmarket.

After a mile you will pass a school on your right. After 2 more miles you will come into Saxtead Green along a road with wide verges. The old Mill House pub is on your left just before you reach the A1120. **Bear R** at the little triangle and cross the main road and take the track to the splendid windmill.

When you have had a look at the mill stand with your back to it and **turn R** onto the A1120, which you are facing. You are only going to be on it for a few hundred yards.

Turn L at the first turning and then **L** again at the small T-junction. After another mile **turn R** at the next junction and carry straight on towards Kettleburgh. As you come into Kettleburgh **turn R** up Church Road. Continue past the 'Private Road'

Framlingham Castle.

notice and up to a group of old houses. The church is behind these on the right-hand side, and well worth looking at.

Return down Church Road and **turn R** and into Kettleburgh. **Turn L** at the T-junction and then **R** over the bridge and continue to Hoo. **Turn L** at the next junction towards Letheringham.

After a mile you will see a church and a red brick gatehouse set in a red brick wall on your right. This is a former priory. Your best way in is to continue past the farm whose yard it adjoins and **turn R** at the next junction. On the corner you will see a path signposted towards the church.

Continue from here past watery meadows along the side of Easton Farm Park. Then **turn R** towards Wickham Market.

When you meet the B1078 **turn L** and this road will take you into Wickham Market. As

you reach the built-up area look out for Broad Street on your right. **Turn R** into it and you will ride straight into Wickham's little square. The church is on the far side of the square.

Take Broad Street again when you leave, signposted towards Easton. **Turn L** onto the B1078 and then **turn R**, heading for Easton, a village worth pausing in for the White Horse pub and the crinkle crankle wall that reaches round the church and along the road, marking the edge of the former Easton Park. Note the connections with foxhunting: the village sign, the kennels and a road named Harriers Way.

Take the **next L turn** to see the entrance of Easton Farm Park. This park has many species of animals and would be worth visiting on a day when you have time to look round properly.

When you leave Easton Farm Park go back

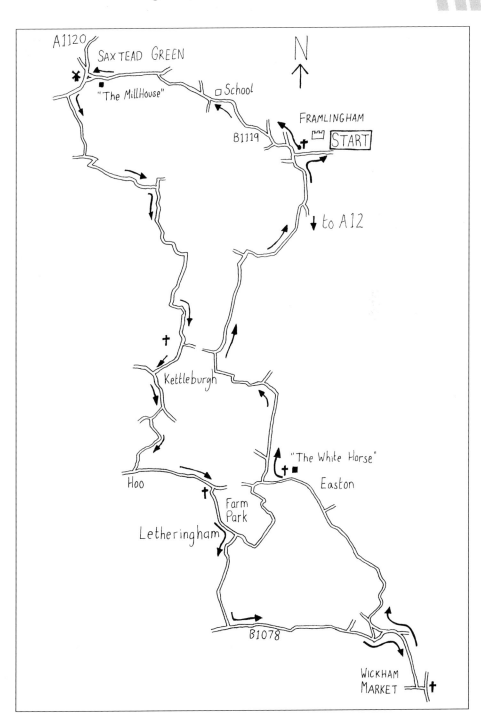

the way you came, towards Easton, but take the first **turn L** towards Framlingham and then the second small turning to **the L** towards Kettleburgh. After another mile **turn R** towards Framlingham.

When you join the B1116 **turn L** onto it and continue into the centre of Framlingham. **Bear R** at the junction and then **R again** and you will reach the main square.

FRAMLINGHAM

Framlingham is a market town compact enough to be explored quickly but with enough features to make you want to return, such as the back of the Queen's Head where bears and their masters used to sleep and the Unitarian chapel with its separate entrances for men and women. The Market Square slopes steeply and contains numerous interesting and ancient buildings. The church has some amazing tombs, including one of a duke who was sentenced to death by Henry VIII but was reprieved only hours before he was due to be beheaded because the King died the previous night. The castle has the Lanman Museum built inside it. It replaces an earlier castle, was completed in 1199 and considered to be a state-of-the-art fortress. It still looks magnificent.

SAXTEAD MILL

The windmill that stood here in 1287 would have ground the corn for the lords of Framlingham Castle. The white painted weatherboarded post mill that stands there now was built in 1706 and still operates. It is in a lovely setting on Saxtead Green not too far from the Old Mill House pub. Check the opening times so that you can look around and take a tour guided by a tape-recording.

WICKHAM MARKET

Wickham Market has not had a market for 300 years but still has a market square. This little town grew up around the bridge and ford across the River Deben used by travellers en route between Ipswich and Yarmouth. The church's tall spire advertises Wickham as you approach, and when you arrive you'll find a couple of pubs and a tea room. Quilters Haven is an unusual shop and worth looking at even if you are not a quilter. There is often an exhibition of quilts or a demonstration in progress, both of which can inspire weary cyclists.

(16)

Snape, Orford and Ufford

25 miles

This ride runs southwards from Snape parallel with the coast – although saltmarshes and estuaries mean that you hardly see the sea – and then inland and north-eastwards across the coastal heathlands known as The Sandlings. You will start and finish at Snape Maltings where marshes meet music, pass a picture book 12th-century castle keep at Orford, visit a pottery and see the stocks for criminals outside Ufford church. You will ride between flattish sandy fields and woodlands in and out of villages where smugglers smuggled and maltsters malted. This is a ride on the extreme east of England.

Maps: Mostly OS Landranger 156 Saxmundham and Aldeburgh, but also a tiny bit of 169 Ipswich and The Naze area (GR 393574).

Starting point: Snape Maltings, Snape Bridge. This is about 6 miles inland from Aldeburgh, 5 miles from the A12, 15 miles north of Ipswich and 20 miles south of Lowestoft. There is plenty of car parking space at Snape Maltings although it gets very busy in the summer.

At the Maltings there's also a coffee shop and the Plough and Sail for pre- or post-ride refreshments. A good halfway pub stop is the Oyster at Butley.

There are some rises on this route, but few that really deserve to be called hills.

Note: This route overlaps with the Suffolk Coastal Cycle Route, which is marked by yellow signs. Don't get confused or you could end up cycling further afield than you expected.

Stand with your back to Snape Maltings and **turn L**, away from the bridge.

At the first junction, **turn L** towards Iken. After about a mile **turn L** again, still towards Iken. Across the fields to your left you can see over Long Reach which is the wide, muddy estuary of the River Alde.

Keep going and **turn L** again to see the pew-less Iken church which stands on a rise above the river. Then return back down the lane and **turn L**, continuing back along the direction you came from. **Turn L** at the crossroads and keep going straight on towards Orford, ignoring all the turns. Before long you will see the castle and church several miles ahead of you.

When you reach Orford carry straight on towards the quay and reward yourself with a cup of coffee or a drink in one of the pubs there or in the square, or just wander around the little streets. It is certainly worth riding down to the quayside to enjoy the busy river.

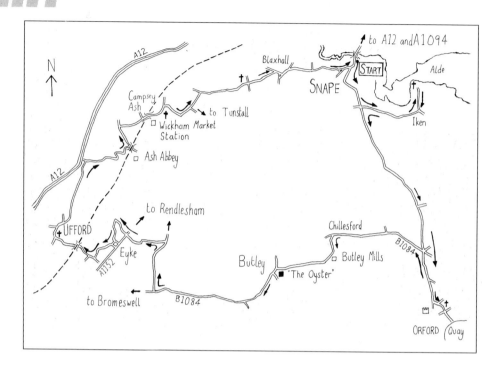

When you are ready to leave Orford, find your way to the castle and, standing with your back to the car park entrance, **turn L** and then **L** again onto the B1084 towards Butley and Woodbridge. After about a mile you will reach a road junction where you should **bear L**.

When you reach Chillesford, **turn L** into a lane which takes you past Butley Mills and on to Butley Pottery Barns on your right. This is a good place to pause to renew your energy. Then continue for a few hundred yards until your little road meets the B1084 again. **Turn L** here and you will see the Oyster pub on your left – an ideal place for lunch or a drink.

Once refreshed, **turn L** along the B1084 towards Bromeswell. Ride for a couple of miles past ancient woodland known as Staverton Thicks. Continue for about 3 miles and then **turn R** towards Rendlesham.

After one mile **turn L** towards Eyke, and continue, **bearing R** at the fork, until you meet the A1152. Cross straight over down a small lane, and continue along here, following a sharp bend to the left.

Follow this lane, **turning R** at the first small junction and then **R** again. Then ride for another half mile until you reach Sink Farm. **Turn R** here towards Ufford.

You will cross the River Deben and a flood plain which used to freeze over and was the site of a spectacular winter Ice Carnival with dancing and ice hockey.

Ride into the centre of Ufford, staying on the same road. Notice the stocks and whipping post outside the church. Inside the church is an amazing font cover – one of the most famous in Europe – but you really need a ladder to appreciate its beauty as it is 18 feet high.

The stocks outside the church at Ufford.

When you come out of the church **turn R** towards Campsey Ash. When you reach the A12 do not cross it but **turn R** and ride through parkland past a mill and the remains of Ash Abbey.

Turn L just before the railway bridge and then **sharp R** away from the drive to Quill Farm. In Campsey Ash you will join the B1078 and pass Wickham Market Station. Just past the church (on your right) follow the road round and on until you reach a bend to the right where you **turn L** towards Blaxhall. Continue and follow the road when it bends sharply to the **R**.

Carry straight on for 2 miles. You will pass a church on your left. **Turn L** when you reach Blaxhall, and follow signs to Snape which is another 2 miles further on.

SNAPE MALTINGS

This was a busy place between about 1850 and 1950 when local barley was turned into malt and shipped to breweries in London and Norwich. It's busy again now because some of its striking red brick buildings have been converted into a concert hall and attractive shops. The concert hall is internationally famous and was founded by the composer Benjamin Britten. On a fine day Snape Maltings is a delightful place where you can lean against your bike on the quayside and look across at the same view of the marshes as the one seen by the maltsters as they leant against their shovels. Or you amble by the river and listen to the call of the seabirds.

ORFORD

Orford is dominated by its 12th-century church and its castle keep – the latter complete with a two-seated latrine. The atmosphere of this little gem of a town is enhanced by the delicious aromas that emerge from the famous Butley

Orford Castle.

Orford Oysterage and The Smoke House where you can eat or buy smoked shellfish, smoked fish, smoked meat, smoked game and even smoked cheese. The craft shop will tempt you to load your bike basket with more baskets, and anyone interested in marine archaeology will enjoy the Dunwich Underwater Exploration Exhibition in the same building. Make sure you go down to the quay. It's a great place to watch people messing about in boats.

BUTLEY

Butley is a small village well worth stopping in. The Oyster has excellent food and beer and tends its oysters only a few miles away in the Butley Creek. Butley Pottery Barns are a collection of old farm buildings which have been converted into attractive galleries for pottery and paintings. The cafe here is an ideal place for lunch if you don't want to go to a pub.

17

Cavendish and Clare

21 miles

This circular route begins with two of Suffolk's most attractive villages – Cavendish and Clare – in the valley of the river Stour, before heading down into the north Essex countryside. Cavendish has all the ingredients of a traditional English village: a central green, thatched pink cottages, pubs and an ancient church. Clare has castle ruins whose ramparts you can walk around. En route you will enjoy panoramas over open rolling fields and glimpses of village life now and as it once was. You will understand why the three Belchamps – Belchamp Walter, Belchamp Otten and Belchamp St Paul – were named as *bels champs*, or beautiful fields, by the Normans.

This ride will introduce you to some special churches which you might want to explore, such as the one in Foxearth with its castle-like tower or the one in Belchamp Walter with its tortoise stove and 14th-century murals. Or you might prefer just to note them as recurring and taken-for-granted features in the distance, reminders of the former power and importance of the church.

Map: OS Landranger 155 Bury St Edmunds Sudbury and Stowmarket (GR 805465).

Starting point: Cavendish village green. Cavendish is about 5 miles north-west of Sudbury on the A1092 and the green is beside this main road in the centre of the village.

In Clare you'll see the Nethergate Brewery whose beer you should seek in the Swan and the Bell. Near Cavendish green there are three pubs, the Bull, the Five Bells and the George as well as several tea shops. The coffee shop in the Sue Ryder museum has a beautiful garden.

This is not an onerous ride and it is only just over 20 miles – not far at all. Be prepared for some ups and downs especially the hill out of Cavendish which you'll meet first at the beginning of the day when you are fresh and again at the end when you can freewheel down it.

If you have come by car leave it on or near Cavendish green and, as you stand with your back to the church, facing the main road, **turn L** onto the A1092. Don't worry – you won't be on it for long.

Take the **first R turn** towards Pentlow and

you will cross over the Stour. **Turn R** towards Belchamp St Paul and up a hill.

At the junction by Forge Corner in Pentlow **turn R**. Continue along here, turning sharply at Paines Manor and then **turn R** at the T-junction.

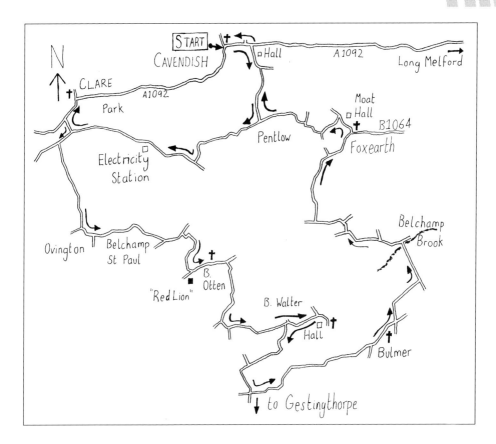

Ride along here for a couple of miles towards Clare, past the electricity station and down Hickford Hill.

Turn R at the turn towards Clare and you will pass the entrance to Clare Priory.

Turn R on the A1092 into the centre of Clare, noting this point to which you need to return. It is worth exploring Clare, especially the church and Country Park. When you are ready to leave, go back to the same point on the A1092 and **turn L** onto the road you were on but then **turn R** at the T-junction.

Then **turn L** towards Ovington and then **L** towards the Belchamps. Ride into the middle

of Belchamp St Paul and **turn L** here by the bus shelter. Go past the post office on your left and then **turn R** towards Belchamp Otten.

In Belchamp Otten look out for Fowes Lane if you want a nice pub. The Red Lion is hidden down here. You will pass the church on your left-hand side and then **turn R** towards Belchamp Walter. Continue along this winding road for about 3 miles, following signs to Belchamp Walter and **bearing left** at the fork. In Belchamp Walter cross straight over the crossroads by a pond and carry on for half a mile.

Then, by a small triangle of grass, carry straight on and down a lane signposted to

Clare's Nethergate Brewery.

Clare church.

the Hall and church. These two buildings seem set apart from modern life in a world of their own. Notice the hounds' heads on top of the Hall's wall and the Slow But Sure combustion burner in the church.

Return to the letterbox on the grass triangle and return up the road back into Belchamp Walter.

Then **turn L** towards Gestingthorpe and **turn L** at the junction. Go uphill and **turn L** at the crossroads towards Bulmer. Ride along here for about three miles.

In Bulmer **turn L** at the crossroads towards the Belchamps down Smeetham Hall Lane and **then L** at the T-junction. After a mile you will cross the small Belchamp Brook. **Turn L** here and keep **L** again, staying on the same road.

Take the **R turn** which is signposted towards Foxearth and Pentlow and **turn R**

onto a bigger road which leads to Foxearth.

In Foxearth **turn R** onto the B1064 for a couple of hundred yards and note the carved foxes on the timbered building on your left. Turn around and ride back – there is another fox on the village sign.

Keep on this road for a few hundred yards, though you may wish to follow the little path past the allotments to see the church with its castle-like tower and amazing Victorian murals.

Turn L opposite Moat Hall and then **turn R** sharply towards Pentlow. In Pentlow there is a pub on the left, down Pinkuah Road. You will also pass a tall, thin tower in the woods on your right.

At Forge Corner **turn R** and ride – downhill this time – back into Cavendish, **turning L** onto the A1092 and back to the green.

One of the many attractive houses in Cavendish.

CAVENDISH

Cavendish is the epitome of a Suffolk village. Its church, 'Hyde Park Corner' almshouses, thatched roofs and sloping green guarantee that most visitors will like it. But this attractive appearance is not the whole truth about Cavendish, as the village sign indicates. In 1381 Wat Tyler, leader of the Peasants' Revolt was killed in London by John Cavendish, son of Sir John Cavendish who was the Lord of Cavendish Manor and Chief Justice of England. The avenging peasants sought Sir John out, chased him and finally beheaded him in the market place in Bury St Edmunds. In the 1650s the church had its windows smashed by Puritans determined to demolish images of God. And less than 200 years ago the games of village football that were held in the High Street had a reputation for being extremely wild and unruly.

The Sue Ryder museum provokes sombre memories of recent European pain and conflict, but refreshments are available in the Sue Ryder coffee shop and its peaceful gardens, and Cavendish has a choice of other pubs and tea rooms.

CLARE

In prehistoric times Clare was a camp sited by an important river. Later the Romans used it as a fortress between the land belonging to the East Angles and that belonging to the Saxons. In the 14th century life in Clare revolved round Clare Castle, which was home (and work) for 250 people, although it was not lived in after the end of the 14th century. In the 16th century Clare thrived on the wealth generated by the wool trade which enabled the large church and some particularly handsome houses to be built. In 1863 the railway came to Clare. The former station and some of the track can still be seen in Clare Country Park from where you can also climb up the castle mound for a good view.

(18)

The Shotley Peninsula

22 miles

This is a ride that features plenty of boats and water. The Shotley Peninsula lies just south of Ipswich between the River Orwell and the River Stour. The ride takes you first past Alton Water, a beautiful, established man-made reservoir with sailing boats and water birds. Then you'll have views across fields to the Stour and its slow traffic which, if you are lucky, may include traditional Thames barges with their rust-coloured sails. At Shotley Gate, the most easterly point of the ride, you will be in Suffolk looking across the harbour to the port of Harwich in Essex and to the North Sea beyond Felixstowe.

This splendid ride has a particularly good selection of pubs that will tempt you to linger by the waterside.

Map: OS Landranger 169 Ipswich and The Naze area (GR 156353).

Starting point: Alton Water Visitor Centre, near Stutton. This is situated about 10 miles south of Ipswich and is signposted from the A137.

There is a cafe at Alton Water Visitor Centre, and the best places to stop for refreshments are at Shotley and Pin Mill, but there are plenty of other pubs en route.

The landscape here is gentle on the whole, but there are a few hills – none too strenuous to walk up if you don't feel like cycling up, and some even go down.

Leave the car park and ride out onto the public road which is the B1080. **Turn L** onto it towards Holbrook.

After one mile you will reach the Royal Hospital School (on the right) and cannot miss its imposing tower and neo-Georgian facade. It was built in 1712 for the orphans of sailors and the children of wounded sailors. Note the Indian princeling figurehead of HMS *Ganges*, a name which will feature again in this ride.

You will pass Holbrook Mill on your right. Then **turn R** and go up Back Hill.

Turn R at the T-junction and ride for a mile into Lower Holbrook. Carry on towards Harkstead and you will come to the Baker's Arms on your right. Don't miss the outstanding views of the Stour to the right – the river will go in and out of sight as the terrain changes.

Keep going towards Erwarton between undulating fields. When you reach Erwarton you'll come to the Queen's Head pub on the left and the church and almshouses on the right. It is said that within the church walls there is a casket which contained the heart of Anne Boleyn, one of Henry VIII's wives and victims.

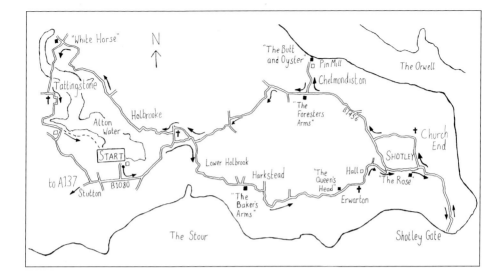

A little further along the route you will pass a splendid red brick gatehouse standing in front of Erwarton Hall. The original Tudor hall was rebuilt in red brick in 1575 and is a fine building.

Continue towards Shotley until you meet the B1456, where you **turn R**.

Ride through Shotley, past the Rose pub on the right, and so down to Shotley gate. As you enter the built-up area keep an eye to the left for the former land based naval training centre, HMS *Ganges*, now used by the Suffolk Constabulary. The mast still stands in the courtyard.

When you reach Shotley Gate take time to get your bearings. You can see the buildings in the port of Harwich opposite with the port of Felixstowe to the left. **Turn L** past the Bristol pub to find the marina, an ideal place for a break.

Once you are ready to leave, retrace your route from Shotley Gate and ride back up the B1456 towards Shotley and Chelmondiston.

Turn R to Shotley church to avoid a couple of miles of the B1456 which can be busy. **Turn L** at Church End and when you meet the main road again, **turn R**.

A few miles further on, as you come into Chelmondiston, **turn R** to Pin Mill just before the Foresters Arms.

Ride down hill past beautiful little cottages on your left until you reach Pin Mill which consists of a small group of houses, the Butt and Oyster pub, the River Orwell, mud and boats. This too is a place worth pausing in.

Leave Pin Mill by the same road (uphill this time) and then **turn R** onto the B1456. Ignore the first turn to your left but **turn L** at the second one, signposted to Holbrook.

Ride along here and **turn L** at the T-junction. At the next junction **turn R**, still towards Holbrook.

At the next T-junction **turn R** and you will meet the B1080. **Turn L** here, into Holbrook.

Bike park at Pin Mill.

Erwarton Hall.

Take the first **turn R** to Tattingstone opposite the church, **turning R** again after about one mile.

Then there is a fairly straight ride for a few miles. Follow the road around a bend and **turn L** at the T-junction. The road now turns to the left but note the White Horse pub ahead which, since Alton Water was created, now stands on a road to nowhere.

Ride down and across Lemons' Hill Bridge and the reservoir – a lovely ride.

You will come into Tattingstone past the now disused hospital which was originally a workhouse with its own burial area.

Turn L past the tiny Orange Box pub and the art gallery next door. Follow the road around Alton Water until you reach the house which looks like a church and is known as the Tattingstone Wonder. It was built by the local squire who needed new workers' cottages but whose wife wanted to be able to see a church from her windows.

Turn L here by the car park and access point to the pathway round the reservoir. **Turn R** onto the path and enjoy excellent views with no traffic other than pedestrians and bikes.

Keep going for a couple of miles until you reach Alton Water Visitors Centre.

ALTON WATER

This reservoir supplies Ipswich with water and was built in 1978 by flooding a valley containing the ancient moated Tattingstone Hall, copses, cottages and farmhouses. Now it is a peaceful scene where water birds congregate. The Visitor Centre hires out bikes and has a pleasant café where you can sit while you watch windsurfers and sailing boats. A path for walkers and cyclists encircles Alton Water and makes for an enjoyable ride.

The pub at Pin Mill.

SHOTLEY GATE

Shotley Gate is where the Rivers Stour and Orwell meet each other and the North Sea. It is the most nautical of places: there's the marina, the harbour, busy docks opposite and the Shipwreck pub and cafe as well as the chandler's shop where you can buy everything from rope to navigation charts. In addition there is the excellent HMS *Ganges* museum which gives a vivid picture of what naval training used to be like. You can easily spend half an hour leaning over the rail by the busy lock and watching boats enter and leave the marina.

PIN MILL

Pin Mill is a small, special village by the edge of the River Orwell. The elegant Orwell Bridge with its steady traffic is within sight, but Pin Mill feels miles away from the ordinary world. As you approach it you will ride straight downhill towards the river with its backdrop of wooded slopes. To the right, the Butt and Oyster pub is washed by muddy tides. It has served honest and not so honest river and sea traders for several hundred years and still has old red tiles on the floor and still serves sailors, though few of them earn a living from their sailing these days. At Pin Mill you can always see boats at anchor, at moorings and coming and going, but the year's most spectacular event is the Annual Barge Match when you can get an idea of what river traffic once looked like. If you have time, take a stroll along the shore in either direction before setting off again.

19

CONSTABLE COUNTRY:
Flatford Mill, Nayland and Polstead

25 miles

This ride takes you through Constable Country in Suffolk, just north of the Essex border. Even if you don't know the work of John Constable, the famous 18th-century painter, it is easy to look at landscapes with an artist's eye as you note timbered manor houses, rivers, sweeping fields and wide skies. The ride is punctuated with crossings over the River Stour and its two tributaries the Box and the Brett. Sometimes you will have views across them and sometimes you will ride through little leafy tunnels on roads speckled with sunlight on summer days.

If you spend even a short time off your bike wandering around the streets full of half timbered houses in East Bergholt, Nayland, Stoke-by-Nayland and Polstead you will be well rewarded. These are beautiful places separated by fields and woodlands, small lanes and slow streams. You may be tempted to come back with a sketch book, or even a fishing rod.

Maps: Almost entirely OS Landranger 155 Bury St Edmunds, Sudbury and Stowmarket but also a tiny part of 168 Colchester, Hadleigh and The Blackwater area (GR 076336).

Starting point: Flatford Mill, near East Bergholt. This is situated about halfway between Ipswich and Colchester (about 12 miles from each), near the B1070, a few miles from the A12.

There is a cafe at Flatford Mill and plenty of places for drinks and lunches at Stoke-by-Nayland, Nayland and at Polstead.

Because of the rivers there are a few valleys, which means that this ride has some proper hills. Don't let these put you off for they will provide you with some stunning views.

Leave the car park at Flatford Mill and ride out and **turn L** onto a one-way road. Almost immediately you will be able to see right across the Stour valley to your left.

You will come into East Bergholt. **Turn L** at the T-junction by the distinctive church. Stop here and take a look at the bell cage in the churchyard; these bells are unusual in that they are hung at ground level, apparently because the completed tower was lower than expected. Keep on riding in the same direction straight through East Bergholt, looking out for the sign above a shop that says 'Dealer in Hatts'.

Ignore the roads leading off on your left, and then **turn L** onto the road by the Carriers

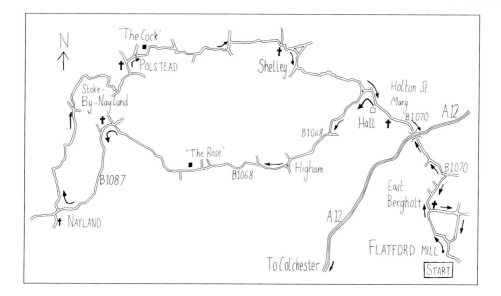

pub, signposted to Hadleigh, and on past the Beehive.

This is the B1070 and is signposted to Holton St Mary. Follow it under the A12 and into Holton St Mary.

Soon after passing Holton Hall on your left, **turn L** on a bend towards Higham and Shelley and then **bear L** at the triangle of grass. Follow along here for a good mile until the T-junction, where you **turn R** towards Higham and Stoke-by-Nayland.

Keep going along here – this is the B1068. Just past Higham you will go downhill and across the River Brett.

Then you will go through Thorington Street, with the Rose pub on your right. Continue on an upwards slope for a couple of miles until you reach Stoke-by-Nayland. There are some beautiful old buildings here including the Crown, the Angel and the Black Horse, but remember that you are not halfway yet.

Turn L at the crossroads towards Nayland,

along the B1087, but pause at the church which is set in a broad churchyard that overlooks gardens. The church door is like a weathered tree and is carved with an amazing Tree of Jesse design.

You can swoop down the B1087 into Nayland, past the invisible site of the former Tendring Hall, home of generations of lords of the manor. When you enter Nayland note Gravel Hill, a small turning to your right, because you need to return to it.

Take your time here and enjoy walking around for a while. In the church there is an original Constable behind the altar, so now's the chance to see one if you haven't had the opportunity before.

If you walk or ride a little way further along Bear Street (the B1087) you will see the Nayland Horse Watering on your left, an ancient stopping place where travellers, their horses and their stock used to drink from the river. You may prefer to try the White Hart.

Return into the centre of Nayland and go

Flatford Mill.

back to where you came in and **turn L** up Gravel Hill, which is a real hill. Keep going for over 2 miles until you reach a crossroads. Go straight across towards Stoke Tye.

This is an attractive little route, albeit with ups and downs, which will bring you to a T-junction. **Turn L** and go past the mill on the River Box. Follow this road round a sharp left-hand bend.

Keep on this road and you will see Polstead church on your left. **Turn R** towards Polstead, leaving the pond on your left. **Bear R** at the triangle towards Layham. The Cock pub should be on your left.

Turn R at the next junction and after a couple of hundred yards **turn L**. Then **bear L** again at the junction by Shelley Priory Farm and then **L** again towards Shelley and Raydon and almost immediately **R** again.

Follow the road sharply to the right when

you reach Shelley and then **turn sharp L** by the church, over the bridge and **turn R** and **R** again following signs to Holton St Mary.

After half a mile **turn L** towards Holton St Mary. Follow this little road for 2 miles and you will find yourself back at the little triangle of grass you passed earlier in the day. Keep straight on, leaving it on your right, and then **turn R** onto the B1070.

Go back through Holton St Mary, under the A12 again, **turn R** onto Hadleigh Road into East Bergholt, **turn L** at the T-junction, go through the town and past the church until you see the signs for Flatford Mill. **Turn R** and follow the one way system round until you reach Flatford Mill car park.

FLATFORD MILL

Flatford Mill, made famous when John Constable painted it, is now a centre for arts and crafts courses and is not open to the public. But you can walk along the riverside, visit Bridge Cottage and see Willy Lott's Cottage – another of Constable's subjects. You can also hire a rowing boat and enjoy the tea room, the shop and the museum, which is particularly worth a visit because of its fine collection of old bikes.

NAYLAND

It is worth spending time in Nayland and enjoying Alston Court and the Guildhall in the main street. The gardens behind the cottages in Fen Street lead to the water's edge. St James's church has roses growing by its walls and over its porch, and Constable's *Christ Blessing the Bread and Wine* above the altar. Nayland seems the epitome of rural life now but once, when it had substantial wool and cloth making industries, it was England's 45th biggest town. Its original wooden bridge over the Stour divided Suffolk and Essex and was constructed in the 15th century. Later on John Abel, who had become rich through the clothing industry, had a hump-backed brick bridge built so that river traffic could reach the mill. Look for his initial on the present bridge.

POLSTEAD

Polstead looks peaceful today – a traditional attractive Suffolk village. On the opposite side of the road from the pond are the church and Polstead Hall. There is also a famous and many centuries-old tree, the Gospel Oak, whose remains are still visible. But where quiet fishermen now stand round the pond, once cruel persecutors watched to see what happened when they tried women accused of being witches by throwing them into the water. Those who swam were guilty, while those who sank were presumably drowned by their innocence. Another story connected with Polstead is the murder of Maria Marten by her lover in the Red Barn in 1837. If all this seems unbearably gruesome, refresh your spirits in the Cock.

20

Haverhill and Finchingfield

21 miles

This ride starts in Suffolk, has a brief encounter with Cambridgeshire and then goes into Essex. It takes you through wide, green landscape that proves that the media's image of Essex as an uninteresting area not far from London is totally false. You will also visit Steeple Bumpstead, Helions Bumpstead and Finchingfield. Ride downhill (mostly) and south from Haverhill and on through rolling countryside and then take time out in photogenic Finchingfield. Its village pond, pub, tearooms, and windmill may well delay you. This ride is perfect for people who like simple routes. It's nearly all straight on.

Maps: Mostly OS Landranger 167 Chelmsford, but a little of OS Landranger 154 Cambridge and Newmarket (GR 675455).

Starting point: Haverhill, which is about 15 miles south east of Cambridge on the A1307. There are various car parks close to the town centre.

Haverhill does not have much of a choice of eating places, but you'll pass pubs in Steeple Bumpstead and Cornish Hall End. However, Finchingfield is the half way point and has all sorts of good places, for there's a pub, a place for tea, another for coffee and a special patisserie.

This ride is really two long straight rides, one going south and one returning north, so you won't have to keep referring to the map. There are some hills but it is a fairly steady, undemanding ride.

Find your way from your car park to the A143 leading in the direction of Sudbury and Halstead. Ride along it until you reach a small roundabout just before the road goes under a bridge. **Turn R** here onto the B1057 towards Steeple Bumpstead.

Ride on for a while until you come to another roundabout where the road you are on meets the A1017. Cross straight over and out onto sweeps of clear countryside.

After a mile and a half you will reach Steeple Bumpstead. **Turn R** here into the village and then **L** over Claywell Bridge.

You need to **turn R** here, following signs to Finchingfield, but make time to explore this village. You'll pass the Fox and Hounds, but you can also find fords, the Red Lion and a pottery if you look around.

Turn R by the half timbered Moot Hall and stay on the B1057 all the way to Finchingfield – about 5 or 6 miles.

You will go through Cornish Hall End, where the redbrick church is on your left, and the Horse and Groom pub on your right.

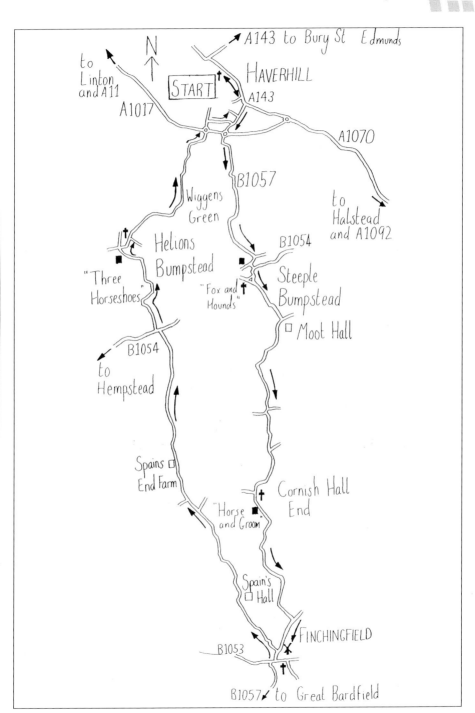

A refreshment stop in Finchingfield.

As you come into Finchingfield **turn sharp R** and you will ride in past the windmill. Note the turning to your right towards Helions Bumpstead which you will take when you are ready to leave Finchingfield.

But take your time here, for, like many others, you will probably find the village very attractive. You'll find everything you want to see within a few minutes' walk. When you are ready to leave go back up towards the windmill and **turn L** on the road signposted to Helions Bumpstead.

You have another straight ride for about 6 miles to Helions Bumpstead. You'll pass the magnificent Spain's Hall on your right. Note too Spains End Farm further on on the left.

When you reach the B1054 cross almost straight over and continue into Helions Bumpstead. Pass the Three Horseshoes on your left and **turn R** at the crossroads, up past the church, towards Haverhill.

Follow the road round through Wiggens Green and on until you reach a roundabout where your road meets the A1017. Cross straight over and **turn R** at the first turning.

Then **turn L** onto the road that leads you back onto the small roundabout on the A143, where you **turn L** again.

FINCHINGFIELD

Finchingfield has all the ingredients of a proper village, and they are all gathered around the green so you hardly have to walk more than a few yards for whatever it is you want to do: feed the ducks, eat an ice cream, admire traditional buildings, browse amongst antiques, have a beer or eat delicious pastries. You can even buy a cuckoo clock. But in 1621 William Kempe did not find Finchingfield congenial. Apparently he accused his wife of infidelity. On finding out that he was wrong he resorted to self imposed silence and shut himself away in his home at Spain's Hall.

SPAIN'S HALL

This Elizabethan brick built manor was built in 1585 and it looks to the passing cyclist as if life there could have been good. But William Kempe gloomily marked each of the seven years of his silence by excavating fishponds in the gardens. His unnatural lifestyle finally had the effect of robbing him not only of the power of speech but of the will to live.

Although today the Hall is occupied by a private family it is open to visitors on occasions when you are shown round parts of the interior by a butler. Outside you can see the remaining two fishponds, now united into one. The moral is to be careful when making accusations and even more careful about taking vows in a fit of remorse.

TOURIST INFORMATION CENTRES

Tourist Information Centres are full of useful, up-to-date information for visitors. All of them will provide details of their area and of other areas: opening dates and times of attractions, early closing days of towns, accommodation (TIC staff will make bookings too) and places to hire bikes from. Not all of them are open all year round but if one is closed another should be able to help you.

CAMBRIDGESHIRE
Cambridge	01223 322640
Ely	01353 662062
Huntingdon	01480 388588
Wisbech	01945 583263

ESSEX
Braintree	01376 550066
Chelmsford	01245 283400
Clacton-on-Sea	01255 423400
Colchester	01206 282290
Harwich	01255 506139
Maldon	01621 856503
Saffron Walden	01799 510444

NORFOLK
Diss	01379 650523
*Fakenham	01328 851981
*Great Yarmouth	01493 842195/846345
*Hoveton	01603 782281
Hunstanton	01485 523610
Kings Lynn	01553 763044
*Mundsley	01263 721070
Norwich	01603 666071
*Sheringham	01263 824329
*Walsingham	01328 820510
*Wells-next-the-Sea	01328 710885

SUFFOLK
*Aldeburgh	01728 453637
*Beccles	01502 713196
Bury St Edmunds	01284 764667
Felixstowe	01394 276770
Hadleigh	01483 823824
Ipswich	01473 258070
*Lavenham	01787 248207
Lowestoft	01502 523000/523057
Newmarket	01638 667200
*Southwold	01502 724729/523000
Stowmarket	01449 676800
*Sudbury	01787 881320
Woodbridge	01394 382240

*not open all year round